TEA
BURNING
TOWN

Scene on "Ye Greate Streete" in Greenwich. The hip-roofed house was built in 1760. The other three are all over a hundred and twenty five years old.

TEA
BURNING
TOWN

BEING THE STORY

OF Ancient Greenwich *ON THE* *Cohansey*

IN *West Jersey*

By *JOSEPH S. SICKLER*

PHOTOGRAPHIC ARTWORK BY CHARLES CORDREY

The Greenwich Press
Bridgeton, N.J.
P.O. Box 1062

The Greenwich Press

Reprinted by permission of the
author and the author's agent
Scott Meredith
Literary Agency Inc.
580 Fifth Avenue
New York, New York 10036

Printed by Cowan Printing, Inc.
Bridgeton, New Jersey

Second Printing 1973
This edition consists of two thousand numbered copies
of which 6 are reserved for presentation.

This copy is number _169_

What This Book Is About

A brief history of Greenwich, Cumberland County, New Jersey, founded with its twin town of Salem by John Fenwick in 1675, and seven years older than the neighboring great city of Philadelphia. This volume is designed primarily as a picture book to show the colonial and antique picturesqueness of the place. The supporting text gives in five chapters the history, old houses, prominent figures, anecdotes, etc.; all of which call attention to the fact that, while colonial America may be seen, restored, at Williamsburg, Virginia, it may be viewed in its original and pristine glory only at Greenwich, New Jersey.

In memory of his mother
and of a long line of ancestors
who were born on "Ye Greate Streete"
of Greenwich

And for Sarah Sheppard Hancock,
whose great contribution to this book
is gratefully acknowledged
by the author

JOSEPH S. SICKLER

Contents

FOREWORD

GREENWICH IS COLONIAL AMERICA. Once a thriving port, it is now an almost forgotten village, tranquil and lovely in its antiquity. The proud houses built by the earliest settlers still stand, many of them unchanged, beneath the ancient sycamores and silver maples that line "Ye Greate Streete."

Greenwich has been called the Williamsburg of New Jersey, the main difference being that in Greenwich there has been no restoration. It has known change and the hand of time but little since it was founded in 1675 by John Fenwick. The passage of years has moved so gently over it that one can still walk along the two miles of "Ye Greate Streete" and visualize the village as it was when England's flag flew high above its roof tops in 1749; or stand by the water's edge of Cohansey Creek and envision the days when this was a busy, bustling port of entry where full-rigged ships docked over two centuries ago.

Now, of course, one sees the inevitable filling station, the 7-Up sign on the tavern, a few new houses. But the heart of Greenwich is still a living thing. It is no reconstructed memory.

Conceivably it will never attract a steady stream of sightseers. It is too quiet, too remote, too far off the beaten track. But it is tremendously important to the thoughtful who like their history straight—whose pleasure it is to seek out the places where America first put down her strong and vigorous roots.

It is for them that I have written this simple chronicle.

The village lies almost forgotten in the great press of American civilization, save for a few lines in a history book recalling a tea party prior to the Revolution. Always, it presents its charming, colonial facade to those who care to see it.

Mute, ancient but not inglorious, here is Greenwich:

"By water's side, on lonely road and village street
'Neath ancient trees whose sheltering branches meet,
Old houses stand, as they stood, long long ago
Each one, a silent witness of life's great ebb and flow."
AUTHOR UNKNOWN.

Beekman Tower
New York City.
March 27, 1949.   Joseph S. Sickler.

Chapter One

OF THE EARLY SETTLEMENT

SELDOM does anyone take the trouble to note that Major John Fenwick, having obtained a grant of land from King Charles the Second, ventured across the high seas to found a little principality in southern New Jersey, in the year 1675. In conjunction with this settlement, which he named New Salem in deference to the peaceful aspect of the place, he planned a second, twin settlement on the banks of the Cohansey, 16 miles from the first. He named this fledgling town, Cohanzick, from the Indian name of the stream, but certain of his settlers, remembering the land from which they came, ruled otherwise and called it Greenwich after Greenwich on the Thames.

Fenwick's dual towns were the first permanent English-speaking settlements on the Delaware River, a fact little noted by historians today. Another all but forgotten fact is that Fenwick by his activities in colonization interested a certain William Penn in American real estate. And to the end that, as Fenwick become involved in financial straits Penn came to the New World, took over in person a large part of the Fenwick holdings and planted a town on the verdant bank of the Delaware which he was pleased to call Philadelphia or the City of Brotherly Love. Yet had it not been for Fenwick's pioneering and subsequent legal difficulties, Penn might not have embarked upon his own venture, which was as magnificently successful as Fenwick's effort was a financial failure. Fenwick

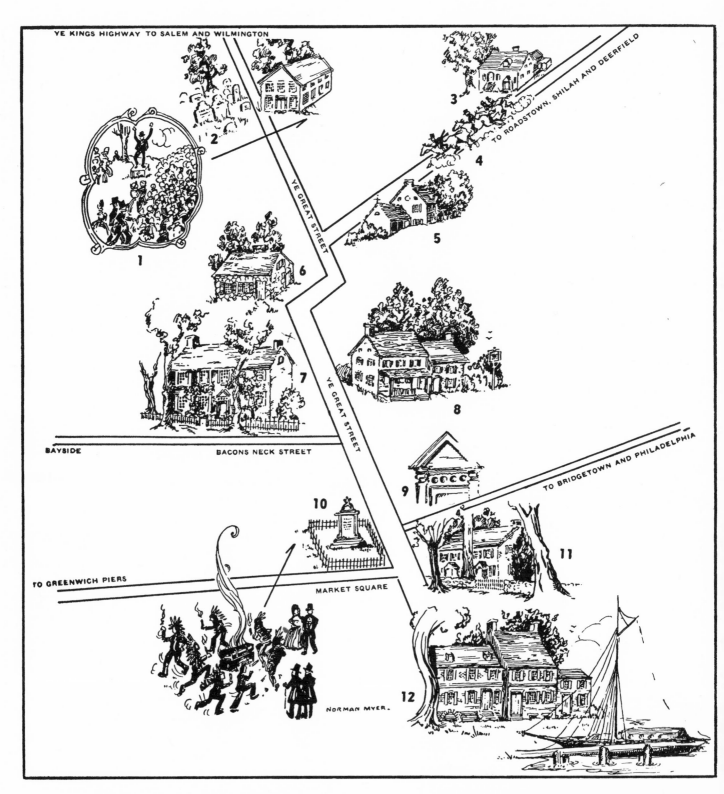

1. *Here, in June of 1740, George Whitefield preached to 3,000 people.*

2. *Presbyterian Church (1835) and old burying ground.*

3. *Howell House (1770), 4 miles from Greenwich, and near Shiloh where the Tea Burners gathered.*

4. *Route of the Tea-Burners' Ride.*

5. *The house of Phillip Vickers Fithian, in which the Tea Burners disguised themselves as Indians.*

6. *Brownstone School House (1811).*

7. *Wood Mansion (1795).*

8. *Stone Tavern (1730). First courthouse of Cumberland County.*

9. *Bull's - Eye doorway. Holmes - Sheppard - Bonham House.*

10. *Tea-Burners' Monument in Market Square.*

11. *Friends Meeting House (1771).*

12. *Sheppard's Ferry House at Cohansey Wharf. Here the* GREYHOUND *anchored on December 12, 1774.*

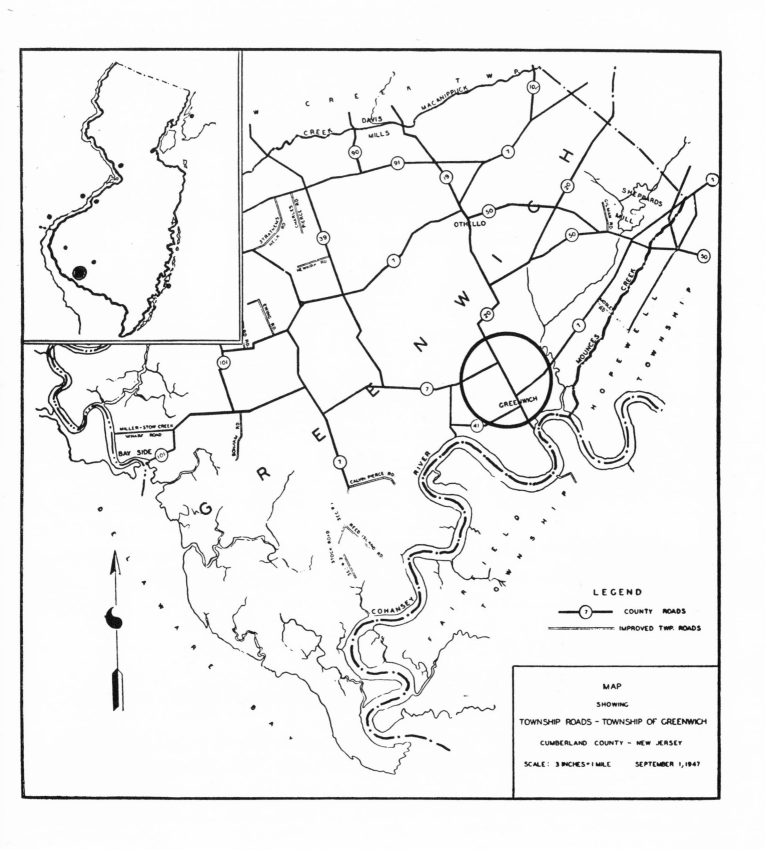

LEGEND

──⑦── COUNTY ROADS

═══════ IMPROVED TWP. ROADS

MAP

SHOWING

TOWNSHIP ROADS - TOWNSHIP OF GREENWICH

CUMBERLAND COUNTY - NEW JERSEY

SCALE: 3 INCHES = 1 MILE   SEPTEMBER 1, 1947

died poor and broken-hearted at the perfidy of his "friends," who he claimed had ruined him in the involved processes of real estate development and speculation. Somewhere in Salem County he sleeps in an unknown grave.

Nevertheless, it is not fair to use the word "failure" in mentioning Fenwick's enterprises. He did build Salem and he did build Greenwich and these two towns, now vastly different, are mighty monuments to him. And we, who come from either of these two towns, may condescendingly look at a Philadelphian and say, "Oh, yes, our home towns are seven years older than yours."

Fenwick's original colony was an elaborate set-up. Not only was it a real estate development, it was also intended as a haven and did attract many Quaker families whose lives had not been too pleasant in England for reasons of intense religious intolerance. The motivation was chiefly material gain, but it must be noted, truly enough, that many took advantage of the prospect to get away from the harsh and hateful persecution to which the English Quakers were subjected.

Fenwick called himself the Lord Proprietor of Fenwick's Colony, and he brought over from England such now obsolete legal instrumentalities as court barons and court leets. He was not only Lord Proprietor; he was Governor as well. He was on the way to maintaining a separate English crown colony which might have been a separate province or perhaps state, in time, when troubles beset him from every side. Lack of money to pay the interest on mortgages, petty jealousies, downright perfidy and treachery on the part of those he trusted, all combined to frustrate his plans for a separate independent colony. Twice, having incurred the mighty wrath of Lord Edmund Andross, Royal Governor of New York, he was dragged out of Salem by soldiers and sent to New York in chains to answer the charge of impersonating a royal governor. He stood up

Interior of Ewing, Bacon, Gallagher House.

Front door of Wood Mansion.

manfully and told Andross off, but he had no real support back of him chiefly due to his financial weakness. His colonists, one by one, deserted him, finally forcing him to sell the greater part of his lands to William Penn and others at ridiculously low sums. The founder died in 1683, after eight years of mental torment and frustration, and others reaped his harvest. His proud little principality of Fenwick's Colony was gathered up and incorporated into the Province of West New Jersey, but he left behind him two towns that lived, Salem and Greenwich.

Geographically, Fenwick's domain lay on the eastern bank of the Delaware River. It ran from Oldman's Creek on the north, to West, or Jehack's, Creek on the south; but the proprietor changed the names of these respective streams to Berkely River after Lord Berkely, his predecessor in title, and to Tweed, indicative of the boundary line between Scotland and England. His names, like Monmouth River for the present Alloways Creek, have been lost with the years. The tract comprised the two present counties of Salem and Cumberland with an area of 1,042 square miles. The grant may be more easily visualized today, as roughly beginning opposite the city of Wilmington, Delaware, and extending southward almost to Cape May. On January 19, 1747-48 (old style) the colony, then called Salem County, was divided in two, the lower part being named Cumberland in honor of the King's brother, the Duke of Cumberland, victor over the Stuart claimant for the throne of England, at Culloden Moor. Greenwich became the county seat, but only for eleven months of that year. An election was then held to determine the shire town. It showed Cohansie Bridge, seven miles to the northeast, easily the victor.

Greenwich, from its position on the Cohansey which finally and tortuously meets the Delaware (six miles to the south of Greenwich), one of the tidal creeks which contributed so much to the colonization of the Mid-

7

dle Atlantic section, early in its career assumed a position of great importance in the shipping trade. As early as 1687, it became a port of entry. Ships, large and small, carried such articles as staves, deer skins, pelts, cedar posts, shingles, wheat, corn, beef and tallow to the growing ports of Amboy Town (now Perth Amboy) and New York, for export to British possessions such as Bermuda and the Barbadoes. In return there came to Greenwich finished wares and merchandise which contributed greatly to the welfare and even the luxury of its people. Salem was a port of entry in 1682, only five years before.

The earliest settlers of Greenwich were divided into two classes: those who came with Fenwick or by his influence, direct from England; and those who came from New England and Long Island. The first group were Quakers; the second Presbyterians and Baptists.

Fenwick planned his twin towns at the same time, 1675. Salem was immediately laid out along its one main street, Broadway, on either side of which 16-acre town lots were sold. Greenwich was not as quickly laid out or settled. This was largely because of rifts between Fenwick and his colonists, and a whispering campaign that his title was not clear. Thus, bedeviled, worried and harassed, Fenwick had little time to perfect his plans for laying out Greenwich as completely as he desired. However, the town was settled in part at least before his death in 1683, and some large tracts were sold; one, for example, Bacon's Adventure of 260 acres, was sold in 1682. Fenwick's will provided for the laying out of Greenwich by his executors. This time it was done thoroughly and completely. "Ye Greate Street" was laid out in 1684 and, as in the case of Salem, town lots were sold along it. Among the earliest settlers, as gleaned from the sale of tracts and lots, were James Wasse, Joshua Barkstead, John Budd, Robert Hutchinson, George Hazlewood, Cornelius Mason, Edmund Gibbon, Samuel Bacon, Alexander Smith, Thomas Watson, John Clark,

Walnut clock and desk (family pieces) with side and arm chair owned, at one time, by Robert Patterson, Director of the U.S. Mint in Philadelphia, who married Amy Ewing of Greenwich.

Old kitchen in Ewing Home.

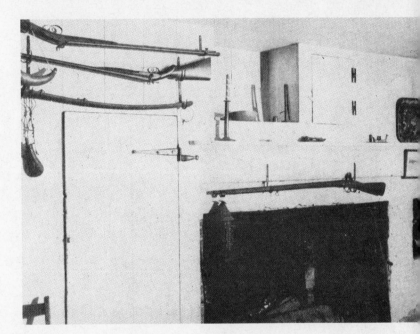

Curly maple bed (Ewing family piece).

China closet in Gibbon House.

Cupboard in Gibbon House.

Nine-foot open fireplace in Gibbon House.

Rear view of Charles Ewing House.

Vauxhall Gardens — Ancestral home of the Maskells.

John Mason, Thomas Smith, William Bacon, Joseph Brown, Edward Hurlburt, Joseph Dennis, Enoch Moore, Obadiah Holme, Mark Reeve and Francis Alexander.

After Fenwick's death his colony passed into the hands of the Proprietors of West Jersey, a real estate holding company that is still in existence. The colony was added to the other tenths, or parts, of West Jersey and a similar arrangement was formed by the Proprietors of East Jersey who have also kept up their corporate existence and hold annual meetings. The records of the first named are kept at Burlington, the second at Perth Amboy. This corporation is undoubtedly one of the oldest in the United States. In certain undeveloped sections of the state there are still tracts of land owned by either division of the corporation.

In less than a decade after Fenwick died, other settlers came to the Greenwich section. Both Baptists and Presbyterians who had found life none too pleasant in New England arrived in fairly large groups. The exact dates are hard to ascertain and are not important. In about 1687, a colony of seventh-day Baptists took up land holdings to the north of Greenwich in the sections now known as Bowentown, Barrett's Run and Shiloh. Other Baptists, who observed Sunday, came to Roadstown and to Greenwich. Their church, known as the "mother church" of South Jersey, was constituted in the 1680's and is today still a flourishing congregation. This is the Roadstown church built in 1803, and still referred to as Old Cohansey.

Simultaneously, the Presbyterians organized a land development society called the West New Jersey Society, not to be confused with the Proprietors, for the purchase of fertile lands along the Cohansey on which their fellow members could settle.

In the early 1690's, a company of men and women from Fairfield, Connecticut, settled on the opposite side of the Cohansey Creek from Greenwich. They called their Presbyterian church, Fairfield, their tiny village, New England Cross Roads. Today, the church still retains its name but the town around it is known as Fairton. At least half of this Fairfield colony immediately crossed the creek and settled in Greenwich. The names of the principal families in this enterprise are listed by the Presbyterian church.

Besides Fairfield, other Connecticut towns were represented by colonists: Simsbury, New Haven, Milford, Guildford and Old Greenwich. There is a controversy over the nomenclature of the town, which will never be settled, as to whether the name is derived from Old Greenwich, Connecticut, or the original Greenwich on the Thames in England. Since Fenwick called it Cohanzick, later spelled Cohansey, it is a good argument in any academic discussion, that since it was changed some one who settled there wished to recall and perpetuate "a" Greenwich.

There is also controversy, even now, as to the pronunciation of the town's name. There are those who call it Gren-itch; others who pronounce it Green-witch; and the third school of expression says Gren-witch.

Motives are naturally of tremendous importance in history. The effects of certain motivation had much to do with the founding of the twin towns, Salem and Greenwich specifically, and with the many, many other towns and cities of the United States of America generally.

Mention was made previously of New Haven, Connecticut. Most American historians have missed completely the fact that, in 1640, colonists from that place resettled at Varkins Kill (now Elsinboro Township, three miles west of the modern city of Salem). Had the New Haven colony survived, it would have been the oldest English-speaking settlement in the three present states of New Jersey, Delaware and Pennsylvania. This was thirty-five years before Fenwick established his twin towns of Salem and Greenwich. The record of this colony is extremely shadowy

---

and very little is definitely known of it. Yet, there is enough to establish a direct chain of motivation for events which happened some years later.

New Haven on the Delaware lasted only from 1640 until 1642-3. Pleurisy, pneumonia, malaria, and the antagonism of their Dutch and Swede neighbors all combined to make life miserable for the New Haven Puritans. Finally in the winter of 1642-3, acting under orders from Kieff, the Dutch governor of New Amsterdam, soldiers swooped down upon the unsuspecting colonists, burned their blockhouse-trading post, and forced them to return to New Haven.

Men do not forget nor forgive when they are evicted from the homes they build or the fields they cultivate. These New Haven colonists had long memories. They had, also, friends and relatives in England. And here, I use the words "Puritan" and "Presbyterian" interchangeably. For this decade of the downfall at Varkin's Kill (now Salem Creek) was also the decade of the English Civil War. In 1649, King Charles the First was beheaded. Thereafter, for ten years, Oliver Cromwell ruled England as a "republican" dictator. The great majority of his army and supporters were Presbyterians. Following Cromwell's death and after it was painfully apparent that his son, Richard, was too weak to wield the power, the son of the late King was, by the offices of General Monk, the Duke of Albemarle, brought over from Breda in Holland, where he had been in exile. He was crowned King under the name of Charles Second.

Among many other things, the new King had to listen to a great number of grievances that had accumulated between 1649 and the date of his restoration, 1660. One of the grievances was that of the New Haven colonists who had lost their lands to the Dutch in 1643.

The royalist or cavalier faction also had a grievance. Strangely enough, by one of those peculiar coincidental quirks of history, at the same time and in the same place (Varkin's Kill) there had been an attempted set-

---

tlement by a fantastic group known as the Knights of New Albion. The leader was Lord Edmund Ployden. One of his chief lieutenants was named Beauchamp Plantagenet, a claimant of royal descent. "Fantastic," because this domain created by King Charles First in 1634 and which extended roughly from New York to Virginia, was a palatinate. With a semi- or quasi-royal government, it included all the high-sounding titles and trappings, such as deputy governors, supreme councils, chancellors, courts of exchequer, courts baron and courts leet, captains general, etc., etc. It was of the nobles, by the nobles and for the nobles. Lord Edmund, the King's Vicar, was the proud father of seventeen children, all of whom he created barons or baronesses in this new kingdom and gave extensive lands. For instance, his eldest child, Barbara was named Baroness of Richneck, an area twenty-four miles wide, adjoining the capital city of Watcessit. It is fairly well established that this empire-on-paper was to have been located in what is now Salem County, New Jersey.

The full title of the colony was the Albion Knights for the Conversion of the Twenty-Three Kings. The Kings were Indians whom the Knights proposed to convert with a sword if no easier method could be found. The Knights went in for heraldry. Much of it for the decoration of the order showed a medal on a riband, and on the medal an open book, The Bible, and a hand grasping a dagger. Also on this medal was a circle in which were twenty-three Indians, all of whom except one had his head cut off, the inference being plain that the one survivor had accepted salvation.

This history is even hazier than that of the New Haven. It is established that Ployden, Plantagenet and a few others came over, established a blockhouse at the mouth of Pennsauken Creek, then came to Varkin's Kill where Lord Ployden demanded and received allegiance from the Puritan settlers. This done, Lord Ployden went back to England in 1640, planning to return. Ployden wanted aid in men and arms, especially for use against the Dutch, from King Charles the First. But that monarch, with a civil war on his hands, could not help him. The war was lost, the king was beheaded, and Ployden died in a debtor's prison. The cavalier influence waned, and the Roundheads, Parliamentarians, Puritans, Presbyterians, call them what you will, took over the reins of governing England. Now the English relatives and friends of the New Haven colonists, their party firmly intrenched in political power, beseeched Oliver Cromwell to aid them in driving out the Dutch in the valleys of the Delaware and Hudson, so they might regain their lands.

Cromwell, however, wanted no trouble with the Dutch because he looked upon them as the strongest Protestant power in Europe. He had inherited a war with them from his royal predecessor, but he absolutely refused to contend with them over American colonization. Also, he had no end of internal strife and bickering to put up with.

But the restoration of the Stuarts in 1660, under King Charles the Second, brought a decided change in the foreign and colonial policy of England. The royalists were clamoring for help; the New Havenists also demanded help. Charles saw that he could keep his own faction quiet, as well as "Jack Presbyter."

A motive that suggested itself to King Charles the Second was the possibility of much material gain by the King and his immediate court from real estate sales. Another was the slave trade. Charles' brother, James, then Duke of York, later King James Second, cast an envious eye on the Dutch who had long enjoyed a preponderance of the Africo-American slave trade. James wanted it for England. He argued long and earnestly with his brother to let him send his fleet to New Amsterdam, seize it for England and cut off, by one fell swoop, the western end of that trade. The third link in the chain of motivation was the persistent plea over a long period of years, with three different English political administrations, by the New Haven Puritan colony and the cavalier Knights of New Albion for the restoration of the lands taken by the Dutch twenty years before. Here and now, Charles could please both sides.

He seized the opportunity. His action changed the history of America and the world. In 1664 a British fleet commanded by Admiral Nichols appeared at New Amsterdam and forced the peglegged Governor, Peter Stuyvesant, to surrender. In honor of the King's brother, the Duke of York, the name of the town was changed to New York.

In recapitulation, partial credit for the English seizure of Dutch territory, including the now vast city of New York, which might conceivably still be under the flag of Holland, goes jointly to the New Haven colony and the Knights of New Albion. And credit must also go to the possibility of material gain from the slave trade and real estate development.

Yet, a decade later, when the colonization of the old Dutch-controlled section began, it was survivors and descendants of the Puritan Connecticut colony who actually moved in on those lush fair lands along the Delaware that their sires had once settled only to lose.

In the years between 1640 and 1690, many Connecticut families crossed Long Island Sound into Long Island. Therefore, from these two sections, new settlers came to Fairfield-Greenwich under the auspices of the Presbyterian West New Jersey Society. For instance, the Fithian family, long prominent in Greenwich history, settled in Easthampton, Long Island, in 1640, and a couple of generations later moved down into the Cohansey section. That there was a family tie between Long Island and Greenwich is exemplified by the case of the Reverend Ebenezer Goold, a Presbyterian pastor at Greenwich in 1740. He did not please his congregation and was dismissed. To quote his own words, he "returneth home to minister the Gospel at Cutchogue in the parish of Southold."

As the colonists prospered, they built the best houses they could afford. The same ships which exported deer skins and pelts brought back nails, laths and other building materials. There is a widespread legend that the ships also brought bricks from England, the same red and blue bricks one still sees in the Greenwich and Salem houses, but this story is very much in error. Though once in a long while a ship may have brought building bricks in ballast from the old country, there were not enough ships afloat in those days to carry all the bricks that went into the construction of the houses in these two towns alone.

No, the bricks were made right on the scene, sand and clay being quite available. To show conclusively that there was a trade, a large one, in brick-making—a West Jersey provincial legislative act passed in 1683 stipulated that all bricks used for construction purposes must be well burnt, of a uniform size and even specified the dimensions: two-and-three-quarters inches thick, four-and-one-half inches broad, and nine-and-one-half inches long. Much speculation and comment have been occasioned by the houses restored at Williamsburg as well as by the present unrestored brick houses as to the blue brick, which in either Flemish or English bond is set with the more familiar red, thus giving a mottled or colored checkerboard effect. The answer to the blue brick is that it was burned "closer," or if you will, "toasted like a marshmallow," fused with the proper kind of wood fuel to give it the vitrified or bluish color.

It is regretted that there is not enough space to elaborate on the brick work of the Greenwich and Salem houses. Suffice it to say that the great authority on the subject is the book, *History Of English Brickwork*, by Nathaniel Lloyd, which traces the transition and development of brick construction and brick design back to the fifteenth century in France and from there to England. The brick designs in colors are most prevalent in the English counties of Kent, Surrey, Sussex and Essex. From these four counties there came to West Jersey artisans who had a practical working knowledge of brickmaking and brick designs. From these English shires come not only the glazed motif but also the diaper and zigzag patterns found on the walls of the Fenwick Colony houses. The bond is simply the laying of the bricks: the two chief designs are called Flemish and English. There were a dozen patterns of bonds used in the English houses, but here only two were extensively employed. The Flemish bond uses an alternate header and stretcher brick in the same course; the English a row of stretcher and then below it a row of header. Technically, the stretcher brick presents the long side to view, while the header shows only the small part, or head. Thus, when a header brick is blue and a stretcher, red, there is presented a wall pattern in red and blue which fascinates the antiquarians. (See below.)

Exterior of the Joseph Hancock House.

Cherry bed in Hancock House.

High-boy. Mahogany, showing Queen Anne influence, cabriole legs, claw feet. In Hancock House.

(Above) Very old pine-top table, mahogany cabriole legs, claw feet. Chippendale chair. In Hancock House.

(Above Right) Mahogany desk; chair (shows strong Queen Anne influence) with cabriole legs, claw feet, shell back, is one of a set of six. In Hancock House.

(Right) China closet in Hancock House.

Mahogany tripod table; old salt-ware tea set; old cups and saucers; Old Empire chairs. In Joseph Hancock House.

It is quite true that Greenwich does not have as many examples of either diaper or zigzag designs on the walls of its houses as does Salem County where this long forgotten art flourished to such proportions as to make the parent shire the leading example of such artistry in this nation. Yet there are enough originals in Greenwich to warrant this description of the ancient English mode of brickmaking and bricklaying.

A note of "modernity" must be added; a very dolorous one to the student of things antique. In the dark years when the appreciation of old things was lacking, say, between 1840 and 1900, many of these fine Greenwich homes had their walls covered with hideous yellow stucco, thus obliterating the priceless designs beneath them. The same thing happened, but fortunately not to such a great extent, in Salem County.

The best way to view Greenwich in its first century of existence (the colonial state), is from the newspaper reports as collected in the Archives of New Jersey. This compiler has therefore selected, quite at random, some of the reports, of varied nature. These give excellent contemporary pictures of the town and of the inhabitants. It is extremely significant to note that there is no account of the tea burning in the press archives; the history of that affair comes only from the Cumberland County court records, from the verbal hand-me-downs of the participants and the one short but highly pertinent note in Fithian's Journal.

The researcher who delves for early Greenwich in the New Jersey Archives has much difficulty in finding the right one. He has the additional task of tracing several Cohansies under which name Greenwich was known for most years of its colonial existence. There are many Greenwich's mentioned. There was one in Gloucester County, now known as East Greenwich Township; one in Sussex (Greenwich Township, Warren County since 1824); there was a Greenwich on Castle Point, long since swallowed up in the city of Hoboken; and there are frequent references to the famous

Greenwich on the New York side, the Village of modern days. There was Greenwich Point opposite Gloucester City, New Jersey; and Greenwich Forge in Sussex County. And in some instances, to add to the confusion, the name is spelled "Grenidge."

The place name, Cohansie, has also had a most peculiar history and evolution. Fenwick named his twin town Cohanzick, after an Indian term. The settlers changed it to Greenwich but it persisted as Cohansie until the Revolution. Fithian repeatedly referred to his home as Cohansie. As the town of Cohansie Bridge, seven miles to the northeast, grew, the name moved there only to lose its identity in 1815 when the county seat became Bridge-town. Today, the "w" is gone and it is simply Bridgeton. The name still applies to the creek which flows past both Bridgeton and Greenwich, but its only other salvage after such a long usage is at a little hamlet on the Salem-Cumberland County line, which is known now as Cohansey. This place is about seven miles northeast of Bridgeton and fully two miles inland from the headwaters of the stream. Cohansey is spelled almost every conceivable way: Cohanzick, Chohansey, Cohanzee, Cohanzey, Kohansey, etc.

The first notice concerning Greenwich in an American newspaper appeared in the *American Weekly Mercury* on December 22, 1724. Oddly enough, this was fifty years to the day before the celebrated tea party. The notice occurred in an advertisement concerning a runaway servant. Advertisements such as this were frequently inserted by irate landowners whose bound or indentured servants made a dash for freedom. In these old and odd accounts the historian incidentally gets a good picture of the sartorial habits of the day.

"Runaway-from Benjamin Davis of Indian Town, (the area near Pine Mount Run) in Salem County near Cohansie, a Servant Man named Edward Jones. . . of tall stature, age about 35 years, having a Scar under one of his eyes, Short Hair, A Sandy Colored Beard, and had on when he went away, an old Home Spun Coat, patched and lined with Blue & Pewter Buttons, no Cuffs, two pairs of Breeches, two Shirts, almost New, one homespun, the other Ozenbrigs, old Shoes, Cap't and a Felt Hat. He has been in the Army and Professes himself a Drummer. Whosoever takes up the said Servant and secures him that his Master may have him again shall have 40 shillings as a Reward and reasonable charges Paid by Me. Benj. Davis."

In 1773, John Peagrum, with the high sounding title of Surveyor General of the Northern District of America, announced in the *Boston Weekly News Letter* the death of John Rolfe, His Majesty's Collector of Customs for the Port of Nova Caesaria alias Choanzey and is pleased to name one Benj. Alford in his place.

There has never been a murder in Greenwich in a span of 275 years. Acts of violence of any nature have been rare, again attesting to the peace-loving proclivities of the settlers and their descendants; the celebrated tea party apparently being the only major exception to this rule.

However, concerning murder there was one account which advertised a murderess as fleeing towards Cohansie. This was in the *Pennsylvania Gazette* for April 24, 1735, and reveals the anguish of a jailor at Freehold, Monmouth County, whose female prisoner got away from him. "Broke out of Freehold Gaol, one Elenor White under sentence of Death for the Murther of her Bastard Child. . . . She is tall and slender, round faced, freckled with Black eyes and Black Hair. . . . Had on when she Broke out Callimoco Gown Striped with red, white and blue and a round eared Cap. She is supposed to have gone towards Cohansie."

In 1742 came a note of mental affliction from the *Pennsylvania Gazette*, "About two weeks ago, one John Leek of Cohansie in West Jersey, after twelve months deliberation made himself a Eunuch (as it is said) for the

Kingdom of Heaven's Sake, having made such a construction upon Matthew 19;12. He is now under Doctor Johnson's care and is in a fair way of doing Well."

In the same year Hugh Blackwood, fuller of the mill on Pine Mount Run advertised for a horse, "lost, strayed or stolen."

The spring of 1736 saw the small pox so prevalent in Salem and in Greenwich that the Board of Freeholders prohibited the holding of the annual fairs for that year, declaring, "affected Philadelphians might bring some of that distemper down with them."

A note of miscegenation appears in the 1738 runaway notice of a reward for Lazarus Kenny. "A swarthy fellow, His Father being a Mulatto and His Mother a White Woman, he is pretty tall and thick set, His Hair is cut off; Had on a felt hat, gray Kersey Coat and Vest, old leather breeches, an old homespun Shirt, Yarn Stockings, roundtoed Shoes and Brass Buckles. He took a large white Stallion that Trots Alltogether, with an old Black Saddle and a Snapped Bridle."

A final runaway notice of the many which filled the colonial newspapers was inserted by Silas Parvin in 1747. "Lost by Runaway, a Negro Man named Sampson, age about 58, and has mixture of Indian blood in him, he is Hip Shot and Goes Very Lame. He has taken away with him a boy named Sam, about 12 to 14 years of age, who was born of an Indian woman and looks very much like an Indian only His Hair. They are both well Cloathed, only the Boy is Barefoot, they have taken with them a Gun and Ammunition and two Ruggs. They both talk Indian very well and it is likely that they have dres't themselves up in Indian Dress and gone for Carolina."

The year 1759 beheld the sad case of John Hall, tavern keeper at Cohansie, who apparently was done in by a city slicker who stole his rum. He laments: "Notice is hereby given that towards the latter end of March last

---

there came to Simon Sparks Ferry at Gloucester, a slender man, His complexion a little bit Sandy, who said he was come for a large Kegg of Jamaica Rum for John Hall, innkeeper at Cohansie, for which the said Sparks delivered himself into his Waggon and as the Spirit has not been carried to the said Hall but thought to be imbezzeled or that some accident has happened to the Waggon by which the Kegg might be Stove and the Spirit lost, if the latter, the said Sparks hereby promises to bear onehalf of the Loss, with the Person that had it, but if carried off, as there is great reason to Suspect it is, any Person informing him where it was carried shall receive five Dollars reward. John Hall."

An observation on the record dry spell in the summer of 1769 came in a letter from William Eldridge to the *Pennsylvania Gazette*. "We have had the most excessive dry spell & Season almost ever known. Our Corn in some Places quite cut off and our Pasture Fields burnt up so that scarce anything green appeared until last Wednesday morning when we had such a Violent Gust that we were almost flooded; wherever the Waters found a descent they ran with such rapidity that Bridges, Mill-Dams, Fences were carried away but happily it did not last long."

Before 1768, travel in and out of Greenwich was entirely by horseback. There was no stage service nearby until September 19th of that year when William Shutt (Shute) advertised a stage waggon which started out in the Stow Creek section, several miles from both Greenwich and Cohansie Bridge but which was the first outlet to the north of Cooper's Ferry, now Camden. The driver made one round trip a week at a rate of three and a half pence a mile, and a flat four shilling charge per person for 100 pounds of baggage. Apparently, Shutt lived at the Stow Creek crossroads and obliged his patrons to come five miles for him rather than he going five miles for them. As a public utility this left much to be desired, so in another three years we find Michael Lee beginning his weekly stage trip to Cooper's Ferry from Roadstown in "a good new waggon, holding twelve persons, the body of which riding on springs, sets out every Tuesday, etc." However, Lee advertised that his stage would attend or pick up passengers for Philadelphia at Greenwich on Monday evenings, preparatory to his departure from Roadstown the next day and deposit such on the Friday following the Thursday of his return from the north. Not long afterwards Lee changed the terminus of the Cumberland stage to leave and depart at the old stone tavern in Greenwich.

By 1774, the stagers had competition by water for a stage boat operated out of Cohansey Bridge,which stopped at Greenwich and went to Philadelphia in a weekly round trip. The boat's rate was five shillings from Cohansie Bridge and 4 shillings and six pence from Greenwich.

David Potter of Cohansie advertised in the *Pennsylvania Packet* for September 14, 1772, that he had "available for hire, a woman with a good breast of milk willing to take a child to nurse." Turning from babies to gambling we find that the reason the Cohansey lottery did not "Draw" on the date advertised in 1772, was that a few tickets more remained to be sold and as soon as they were disposed of, "the Drawing will be held without fail." And back to medicine: Doctor Elijah Bowen advertises to meet all and Sundry who are Afflicted with Cancers or with worms and to "speedily cure same."

The concluding item from the newspaper archives is a naval and wartime item: "TO BE SOLD at vendue in Greenwich, County of Cumberland 11th October 1779, the prize brigantine Sea Horse with her cargo consisting of 1200 bushels of salt, 20 barells of sugar, 10 barells of pork, 6 barells of loaf sugar, 1 pipe of wine, a quantity of apples, tea, turpentine and a variety of other articles By Order of the Court of Admiralty. Joseph Potts. Marshall."

Chapter Two

OF CHURCHES AND OF TEA

THE QUAKERS WERE the first settlers of Greenwich. Their influence is readily perceived by the fact that there still remain two meeting houses of that faith, although the number of members has dwindled considerably and one of the edifices, the Orthodox, is not in use for services. The first meeting was associated with Salem but in 1698 a house was built on the slight elevation overlooking the Cohansey, on the same site as the present Orthodox meeting house. The families who constituted the original Greenwich meeting bore such names as Stewart, Test, Tyler, Bacon, Horner, Dennis, Brick, Sheppard, Wood, Miller, Haines and Reeves. All these names survive today, either in Greenwich or close by.

The Baptists and the Presbyterians came together in the late 1680's and 1690's. The first-named sect with its two divisions of Seventh Day and regular Sunday Baptists settled in and around Roadstown, Bowentown and Shiloh, in territory to the north and east of Greenwich; the Presbyterians came first to Fairfield on the other side of the Cohansey. They named their church, Fairfield, after that place in Connecticut and their new settlement, New England Cross Roads. Soon both faiths penetrated to Greenwich but the Baptist influence was meagre compared to the Presbyterian. As early as 1705, a Presbyterian church was erected, a church destined to be one of the strongest of that faith in the entire colonies and to supply them, the state and the nation with some great names. Some of the families who constituted the first church were named Maskell, Miller, Watson, Ewing, Seeley, Dare, Fithian, Sayre, Sheppard, Moore, Peck, Vickers, Woodruff and Lupton.

From these families came two names destined to rank high in the field of American letters. One was John Fanning Watson, the indefatigable researcher-historian who wrote the Annals of Philadelphia. The other was Phillip Vickers Fithian whose Journal, which was not printed until 1900, was chiefly responsible for the accuracy of the Williamsburg restoration. Fithian, a graduate of Princeton in the class of 1772, became a tutor in the home of the Carter family at Nomini Hall, Westmoreland County, Virginia. Here, his powers of objective observation being marked, he noted not only the social activities and the Virginian mode of living but such details as the number of window panes in a sash, the size, the thickness of the walls, the pattern of the brick work, all of which served as a concise guide for the restoration architects and builders.

For two centuries Greenwich has had no new religious faiths. Following the Revolution the Methodists attempted a congregation, but this lasted only a short time.

As part of the history of the Presbyterian church one of Greenwich's most celebrated events occurred. In fact, it was one of the most sensational happenings in the religious history of the colonies. This was the visit of George Whitefield, renowned English missionary, in 1740. Benjamin Franklin attested to his stupendous oratorical powers and crowd-drawing ability. Franklin reported that crowds gathered on the New Jersey side of the river could hear him distinctly, though he spoke from the Market Street Hill near the waterfront in Philadelphia. In June of that year he spoke at Greenwich, on the approximate site of the present church, and it is said that 3,000 people gathered to hear him. If so, it certainly sets some kind of a colonial record when one considers the scarcity of population and the total lack of transportation facilities in rural districts. Whatever the size of

The schoolhouse.

Friends' Meeting House erected in 1771. Note sign on tree describing edifice. The citizens of Greenwich and the Cumberland County Historical Society have so marked the historic buildings in this section.

Interior of Friends' Meeting House. This house is no longer used for services.

Wharf scene, Cohansey Creek, Greenwich.

the crowd may have been, Whitefield was pleased. He wrote to a friend at Salem: "Yesterday at Cohansey the Spirit of the Lord moved over the whole congregation; we have good reason to be thankful for the great things we both see and hear." Whitefield was part prima donna. Earlier in that year he had been scheduled to speak at Greenwich, but by some error went to East Greenwich in Gloucester County (Now Clarksboro) where he mournfully recorded in his Journal: "There being a mistake in the place where I was to preach, I had not over 1,500 hearers."

In a sense, the history of the Greenwich Presbyterian church was the history of its ministers. The congregation was extremely strong and attracted the very best preachers to be found. Among them were Charles Beatty, Samuel Finley and Gilbert Tennent, men who contributed largely to the founding of the log college on the Neshaminy at Hartsville, Pennsylvania, which later developed into the College of New Jersey or Nassau Hall at Princeton. Also there was John Brainerd, brother of David Brainerd, the latter a celebrated missionary among the New Jersey Indians. Lastly there was Andrew Hunter, one of the great names in the Presbytery of West Jersey. He was definitely one of the ablest ministers of his time and was so loved by his congregation that at his death in 1775, he was buried under the main aisle of the church.

That edifice became dilapidated and was torn down to make way for the new and present church in 1835. This structure was erected on the opposite side of the road; however, the old church may be traced today, in outline, by Hunter's grave.

From 1737 to the Revolution, the Presbyterian church was torn by a rift over fundamentalism. The Fairfield congregation, across the Cohansey, called themselves the "old side," or strict Calvinists, while the Greenwich church and the nearby Deerfield church (twelve miles northeast) espoused the new, or liberal, side. Mingled with this church liberalism was a strong feeling of patriotism, and there is no doubt but that Hunter's congregation was as ardently American in its collective feeling as any colonial church body could be. Practically the entire roster of the tea burners, including Hunter's nephew, of the same name, and the celebrated Philip Vickers Fithian were members of this church.

With marked liberality in religion and in politics, the stage is set for the one great event which brought the name of Greenwich into national prominence and linked it forever in the pages of American history with Boston and Annapolis in the patriotic role of the towns that destroyed the tea.

By 1774, "no taxation without representation," had become a familiar slogan. There were many schemes by which the Tory-controlled British parliament endeavored to tax the American colonies. There was a levy on almost everything; the most familiar examples being tea, stamps and window glass.

Even today, in the Greenwich-Salem section, there may be found innumerable windows, bricked up in the years 1760 to 1775 and still bricked up because the parliament had placed a tax on the number of window panes in a house. Rather than pay this unjust tax, the colonists preferred to do without sunlight and closed up the unnecessary windows.

Then the tax on tea hit the one luxury the Americans were used to and could afford to indulge in. The love of tea they had inherited from their mother country and to have it taxed by a group of heavy-handed politicians infuriated them. Their appeals, in the specific case of the tea tax, falling on deaf ears across the water, the colonists resorted to violence. The Boston tea party was a warning to the British overlords of the unpopularity of their course; the destruction of the tea from the holds of the Dartmouth on December 16, 1773, electrified and thrilled the colonists.

With this one act of defiance, there were bound to be others. On October 18, 1774, the people of Annapolis, Maryland, forced a ship owner named

Stewart to burn his own vessel, the Peggy Stewart, which contained, among imported goods from England several chests of tea. About a week after this conflagration, a certain Phillip Vickers Fithian, erstwhile tutor at the Carter's Nomini Hall in Virginia stopped in that town overnight enroute to his home in the Jersies and heard the details of the burning.

On the night of December 12, 1774, there appeared in the Cohansey Creek a brig named the Greyhound, J. Allen, Captain, with a consignment of tea from the East India Company in London. Some accounts have it that the tea was destined for Philadelphia; others that it was consigned to Salem. At any rate, fearing an approaching northeast storm and the possible wrath of the colonists, Captain Allen "put in" and docked at Greenwich. The pilot at Lewes, Delaware, in bringing the Greyhound up the Delaware, had undoubtedly told Allen, since there was no other earthly way of his getting the intelligence, about the Peggy Stewart affair at Annapolis and also about the fate of the ship Polly, carrying tea, which the citizens of Philadelphia had turned back. They used no violence but simply refused the master, Captain Ayres, permission to unload at that port.

The captain of the Greyhound knew a loyalist named Daniel Bowen, recommended to him previously as "a safe man." To his home (now destroyed) a furlong from the wharf, Allen late that night transferred his load of tea, probably assuring himself that in this peaceful country town his cargo was secure until such time as he could remove it to its consignment port. He was in for a very rude awakening; in transferring the cargo from ship to shore, he committed a serious error.

Sharp eyes saw, and sharper tongues talked. By noon of the 13th it was all over Greenwich and Cumberland County that tea had been landed and stored in the Bowen house. Several days passed, then prominent and patriotically inclined older citizens of Bridgeton, the county seat, announced that there would be an indignation meeting relative to the tea to be held at

---

the court house on Friday, the 23rd. There were many who felt that talk and discussion would be sufficient; there were others who believed in direct action.

Thursday, the 22nd, passed quietly enough, although it is undoubted that beneath the surface of serene and quiet Greenwich, preparing that night for its one date with destiny, there was much excitement.

At sundown several young men might have been noticed going into the home of Richard Howell near Shiloh, about four miles from Greenwich. If one observed closely enough, he would have seen about twenty men come out of that house shortly and ride together down the Greenwich road to the home of Phillip Vickers Fithian.

It was quite dark. Suddenly there was a commotion in the Market Place. Lighted only by flambeaux, mysterious, grotesque figures glided in a long line at single file from Bowen's house, carrying huge chests on their backs. In a very few minutes the flambeaux were not needed. The whole village was alight as crackling flames roared upwards consuming the cargo of the Greyhound whilst around the huge bonfire there danced a score of painted, feathered Indians. The spirit of Boston and Annapolis had come to Greenwich.

One of the youthful teaburners was named Henry Stacks. Before the night was over he had acquired a nickname. It appears that this arsonist was a great lover of tea and even though he joined the band for better or for worse, he had mental reservations about the waste of good oolong. Therefore, on the far outskirts of the pyre, Henry, hoping he was unperceived, surreptitiously gathered up as much tea as his breeches, pockets and coat lining would hold. Then crammed full of tea down to his hose and shoes he became quite overstuffed and literally resembled a walking warehouse. Spotted at this pastime he became forever, "Tea Stacks."

The destruction of the tea, the property of others, caused great consternation in Cumberland County and much mental and financial anguish to the consignees of the tea in Philadelphia. Several attempts were made to prosecute the "Indians" both civilly and criminally for the act. The prosecution for the Crown, incidentally, in the next to last term of a royal court endeavored to indict the men but failed to get a Billa Vera or true bill due to the fact that a majority of the Grand Jury were Whigs and secretly approved of the Indians' action. Then Governor Franklin removed the Whig sheriff, Jonathan Elmer, and put in his place David Bowen, a loyalist who summoned a new Grand Jury with exactly the same results. Following this the irate owners, John Duffield and Stacy Hepburn of Philadelphia, tried a civil action of trespass on the case at the spring term of Cumberland County Courts in 1776. Needless to say, this never came to trial.

There are several lists of the tea burners. There are also several accounts as to how many participated. Some say twenty; others, forty. The list most acceptable to historians and the one which was used in carving the names on the monument of white marble which commemorates the affair and is placed in the center of the Market Square at Greenwich, is that of Colonel Robert Gibbon Johnson, the first historian of Salem County and a grandson of Nicholas Gibbon, of Greenwich. In 1774, there were still resident in Greenwich, some of his cousins. Thus, Johnson from his family connections in the town had a right to know, although he was but four years old at the time. His list is as follows: Ebenezer Elmer, Richard Howell, David Pierson, Stephen Pierson, Silas Whitecar, Timothy Elmer, Andrew Hunter, Junior, Phillip Vickers Fithian, Alexander Moore, Junior, Clarence Parvin, John Hunt, James Hunt, Lewis Howell, Henry Stacks, James Ewing, Thomas Ewing M.D., Josiah Seeley and Joel Fithian.

To this list the late Frank D. Andrews in his brochure on the tea party added the following names: Joel Miller, Ephraim Newcomb, Silas Newcomb, Henry Seeley, Abraham Sheppard and Enos Ewing.

Many of these men became famous: Fithian, Richard Howell, who later was governor of New Jersey; Ebenezer Elmer, a brigadier general; Lewis Howell, twin brother of Richard, who was an officer in the continental line and died of disease on the day of Monmouth Battle; Andrew Hunter, a very eminent Presbyterian divine; Thomas Ewing, a surgeon in both the Army and Navy of the young Republic; Joel Fithian, the first sheriff of the county to be elected by the people; and Silas Newcomb, the general of the famous continental brigade which bears his name. Over this last name there is contention. Some claim that the tea burner was Silas Junior, instead of his father who was at that time a colonel in the New Jersey militia and a veteran of the French and Indian Wars.

The counsel for the "Indians" was Joseph Bloomfield, then practicing law in Bridgeton. Like Howell he became a governor of New Jersey. The large suburban city of Bloomfield in Essex County is named in his honor.

The only literary note on the tea party comes from Fithian's Journal. The naivete of his entry should be taken clearly in account. "Fryday 23 (December 23, 1774). Last Night the Tea was, by a number of persons in disguise taken out of the House and consumed with Fire. Violent and different are the Words about this Uncommon Manouver, among the Inhabitants —Some rave, some curse, and condemn. Some try to reason; many are glad that the tea is destroyed, but almost all disapprove the Manner of Destruction."

The footnote in the 1934 edition of his Journal, published by the Princeton University Press (Albion and Dodson, compilers) says: "In spite of his apparent innocence in these remarks, Fithian is credited with having been a principal at this Greenwich tea party in which the cargo of the brig Greyhound was burned. The monument erected in 1908 to commemorate the event includes his name among the participants."

Chapter Three

OF PHILLIP VICKERS FITHIAN

Pʜɪʟʟɪᴘ ᴠɪᴄᴋᴇʀs ꜰɪᴛʜɪᴀɴ, observer of window pane sizes, reporter of colonial social customs, Presbyterian preacher-missionary, journalist, tea burner, ardent lover by mail, army chaplain, prophet and intense American patriot—was born at Greenwich, December 29, 1747. His parents were Joseph and Hannah Vickers Fithian.

Fithian grew up in the Greenwich-Cohansey section. Early showing an aptitude for books, he was sent to the Presbyterian parsonage at Deerfield to study Latin under the tutorship of the Reverend Enoch Green. Here, at a very early age he met Elizabeth Beatty, a sister of Mrs. Green, and began the romance marked in after years by his fervent letters to "Laura," his name for Miss Beatty. More schooling was obtained from the Reverend Andrew Hunter, minister of his own church at Greenwich. In 1770 he entered Princeton, then more popularly known as Nassau Hall, and graduated in 1772. A classmate, Andrew Hunter, Junior (actually a nephew of the Rev. Andrew Hunter), seems to have been his only close friend and associate in college, for the student Fithian does not seem to have mingled with his other college mates of the time, some of whom are mentioned prominently in American History: Aaron Burr, James Madison, "Light Horse" Harry Lee, Phillip Freneau, Aaron Ogden, Henry Brockholst Livingstone and Morgan Lewis.

Many of his fellow students at Princeton were studying to be Presbyterian ministers; thus it may well be assumed that a rough division could be made into the "serious minded" and the "worldly." Yet, among the first class there were backsliders. Fithian wrote from Princeton to his father as to the conduct of two ministerial students (Wilson and Glover) who were expelled from college, as he puts it, "Not for Sabbath-Breaking, Drunkeness, Fighting, Swearing or Open Lewdness But for stealing Hens." This case intrigued the young student greatly. He calls it, "mean, shameful and unmannerly Conduct." After tearful pleas by fellow students and families the two were reinstated in college. One of them, Wilson, became a noted minister but the other, Glover, "fell from Grace," and the next year was caught stealing "turkees." This time he was expelled for good.

However, Fithian in his college letters (before the days of his Journal), was not unmindful of boyish pranks and the generally accepted fact that boys will usually commit mischief when they get a chance, although he certainly did not condone the world-be preachers who pilfered fowls. He does tell that when in school at Greenwich he put a load of snuff into the mouth of a slooping boy and was soundly flogged by the school master for it. He goes on to admit that he richly deserved the flogging.

There is only one feature of Fithian's college career which deserves serious attention. As far as is known, his commencement essay (September 10, 1772) has missed the notice of political scientists and psychologists. It is labeled, "an Exercise," but it reveals the early maturity of his thinking, even though its style is amateurish, stilted and labored. He begins with the theory that "political jealousy is a laudable passion." He discusses other forms of jealousy: domestic, ecclesiastical and those between friends and the sexes. The last named he boldly admits is "dangerous." But he says, political jealousy is desirable, since "esteem" is the foundation of it, and if a ruler or a government will look around them, see other and better forms of government, then strive "jealously to emulate them," the people of that particu-

Exterior Morris Goodwin House.

Walnut bed in Miss Mary Goodwin's home.

High-boy and chairs in home of Miss Mary Goodwin.

Cupboard in Phillip Vickers Fithian House.

lar land will be happier and better governed. Such a jealousy will "unite the people; it will terrify the spurious, selfish politicians."

He concludes this essay on political science with an apostrophe, one of his favorite modes of writing; "May Heaven Inspire the King. Fill him with boundless Love and Harmony towards his people." The last lines of the apostrophe contain a most significant and prophetic note: "But if it is written in the Book of Fate that a change must take place, transfer it to this Western World, establish Government, set over it men as shall ever be watchful for the common Good, that they may rule forever, a brave, free and happy people."

Upon his graduation from Princeton, he returned to Greenwich where he decided to embark upon a ministerial career and so studied theology under the two friendly pastors, Green and Hunter. After a year, or in the early fall of 1773, he received a letter from Hunter, Junior, who was back at Princeton studying theology, advising him that President John Witherspoon (three years later a signer of the Declaration of Independence) had received a request from "Councillor" Robert Carter of Nomini Hall, Westmoreland County, Virginia, desiring a tutor for his children and offering said Hunter, "Sixty Pounds a Year, a servant, a library and a Room to Study in."

Fithian accepted the offer in Hunter's stead and on October 20th, 1773, rode out of Greenwich for Virginia, which 260 miles he covered in seven days. For an even year he resided at Nomini Hall. Here he began his famous Journal which, incidentally, was to lie unpublished for a hundred and twenty-four years after his death.

Stitled, stiff, ministerial, formal, unwilling to dance or play certain games, he nevertheless got along splendidly with the Carter family. They respected him; he respected them. Mention of great names and of great estates passes through his Journal: Lee, Washington, Curtis, Tayloe, Fairfax, Lee Hall, Stratford, Chantilly, Bushfield, Mount Airy. Invited to all their functions, he attended, indulging not in the revels but always gentlemanly, mannerly, polite. He assisted the ladies from their mounts, held open the entry doors for them and bowed when "occasion demanded it." He wrote all in his book, describing the beauty, the characteristics, the gowns of the young ladies, only to observe at the end of the passage that while they were indeed beautiful, his heart belonged to Elizabeth Beatty.

But he could not forget his rigid Presbyterian training and upbringing. On the one vacation he enjoyed from his schoolmaster labors, he wrote, "In Greenwich, there is some respect for the Sabbath. In Virginia, there is little thought of its sacredness. How unlike (Virginia) . . . The morning vastly pleasant & Cohansie (Greenwich) looks as delightsome as ever it used. No Rings of Beaux chattering before & after Sermon; on Gallantry; no assembling in crowds after Service to dine & bargain; no cool spiritless harangue from the pulpit."

A few instances of his close observations at Nomini Hall will suffice: the most important of which is his recording of the architectural dimensions. After Nomini Hall had been destroyed, the cold facts in Fithian's Journal enabled the restorers of Williamsburg many years later to get the exact dimensions for the planned restoration buildings. He wrote that the Hall was "76 feet long East to West and 14 feet wide North to South, two stories high, the pitch of the lower story being seventeen feet. Precisely, he says, "On the south side or front in the upper story are 4 windows, each having 24 lights of glass—In the lower story are 2 windows each having 42 lights of glass and 2 doors each having 16 lights."

He was just as meticulous in describing the costume of Miss Sally Panton:"Her stays are suited to come up to the upper part of her shoulders, almost to her chin and are swaithed round her as low as they possibly can be, allowing her the Liberty to walk at all. To be sure this is a vastly modern Dress."

Of Miss Jane Washington, he notes: "She appears to-day in a cotton chintz gown with an elegant Blue Stamp, A Sky Blue Quilt, spotted Apron. Her dress is rich and well chosen but not tawdry nor yet too plain. Her hair is a light Brown, it was crap'd up with two Rolls at each side and on the top, a small cap of beautiful gauze and Rich Lace with an artificial flower inter-woven. Her person and carriage resembles not a little my much respected Laura."

Fithian also discovered that girls will be girls, speaking of two of the Carter children: "This day, in the school room Nancy & Fanny had a Fight about a Shoe Brush—Fanny pulled off her shoe, threw it at N. broke a pane of window glass, then entered upon close scratching & which Methods seem instinctive in Women."

Gossip found its way, too, to Nomini Hall. The tutor writes: "It is said that B——was the Ghost which walked in the Nursery last Night. I think the Report is false & arises from Base Calumny."

His tutorship completed at the Carters, Fithian returned home, never to see Tidewater Virginia again. On Sunday the 23rd of October, 1774, he spent the day resting at Annapolis, Maryland. He writes in his Journal, "Teusday (sic) evening the people of this Town & of Baltimore, obliged one Anthony Stewart A Merchant here, to set fire to a Brig of his lately from London in which was seventeen Chests of tea. The People seem indeed to be full of patriotic Fire"—This Brig was the Peggy Stewart and as mentioned in the narration of the tea-burning episode, the forced conflagration prob-ably gave ideas to young Fithian. He arrived in Greenwich two days later and at once applied for admission as a minister of the Presbyterian synod or district of Philadelphia. A few days later, in the old church at Pittsgrove (Daretown, Salem County) which is still standing, Fithian was examined by five clerical examiners, passed and was given a license to preach. One of the five who sat on the Board was Rev. Nehemiah Greenman whose initials one may still behold carved in the brick work of the Daretown church. This was the 6th of December. A certain brig called the Greyhound from Rotterdam with a full cargo of tea was not far off the Delaware capes. On Sunday the 18th, the new minister preached his first sermon at Deerfield, where his future brother-in-law, Enoch Green, was pastor.

Concerning that first sermon. Fithian shows that despite his ego and despite his stiffness, he had a sense of humor, for his Journal says, "I preached my first sermon at Deerfield on Job 23:3.4. . . . I was much frighted in the entry of the Service. And as I was told by a friend afterwards, made a material blunder in the first Prayer, 'desiring of God that the King may become a nursing mother & the Queen a nursing Father to the Church.' " In the same entry as which he confesses the biological error, he adds, "Early last week, A Quantity of Tea said to be shipped at Rotterdam was brought & privately stored at Dan Bowen's in Greenwich—A Pro Tempore Committee was Chosen to secure it till the County Committee be duly elected." On the 22nd he notes "The County met at Cohansie Bridge (now Bridgeton) & Chose a Committee & it was recommended to them to examine into & take proper care of the aforesaid Goods."

While the county committee was talking and planning public meetings, the "Indians" acted and burned the tea.

How much suspicion attached to Fithian as the probable instigator of this destruction will never be known. Although he had property he was not sued. Actually, the alleged participants for whom the Crown unsuccessfully attempted to get indictments and against whom the owners, equally unsuccessfully, sued in trespass on the case, were Joel Miller, Abraham Sheppard, and Ephraim and Silas Newcomb. However, suspected or unsuspected, Fithian remained in Greenwich for two months thereafter then went off on a brief missionary preaching tour into the pine woods of southeastern Jersey. During this tour, on which he preached several sermons at Egg Harbour, Batsto, Sweetwater, Bargaintown, Absecon and May's Landing, he took time out to ride to the seacoast (near the modern Atlantic City) and saw the ocean for the first and last time.

Fithian, although a licensed minister was never ceremoniously ordained. The war and other factors prevented that. In the spring of 1775, Presbyterianism was in full flower in the colonies, especially in the Middle Atlantic section; ministerial competition was strong, pulpits were hard to find, so the policy of the Presbytery was to send out its younger preachers, like Fithian, to the frontier as missionaries. This "frontier" was not actually the last western outpost of civilization, which at that time was Kentucky. But the Shenandoah Valley of Virginia and the Susquehanna of Pennsylvania were wild and remote enough to warrant such an appellation. As a missionary, Fithian began his first western trip in May, just three weeks after the war had broken out in Massachusetts. He went down into the Shenandoah beyond Winchester, then retraced to emerge in Pennsylvania near what is now Mercersburg; from there he went north to Sunbury, Williamsport and Lock Haven; then back and a bit west to Standing Stone (Huntingdon), and from there home.

On October 2nd, 1775, he married his boyhood sweetheart, Elizabeth Beatty, at Mayberry Hill, Snowden Lane, Princeton, in a house that is still standing. President John Witherspoon of the College of New Jersey performed the ceremony.

Three weeks of honeymoon and he was off on his second missionary trip which took him into Virginia again, as far south as Natural Bridge and as far out into the Alleghanies as Warm Springs (now West Virginia). These two trips form the basis for his so-called "second" journal as differentiated from the "first" or Tidewater—Nomini Hall—New Jersey diary. Two editions have been published by his Alma Mater at Princeton—in 1900 and 1934, respectively.

His Journal is tremendously important as it reveals the customs of the times, be they social Tidewater, Calvinistic Greenwich or frontier; it also has the great gift of prophecy and is exceedingly interesting because of what it reveals of Fithian himself. He knew he was writing for posterity; what people might think of him two centuries hence greatly influenced his writing. He confides to his Journal that a minister of the Gospel must be as careful of his reputation as a virgin, to the end that some might think him and call him an "unbearable" snob. Conceited he was, and he cultivated the best people. If his motivation could be dissected, it would probably be found that he chose his career as a preacher because of the social and intellectual position it involved rather than any burning desire for ministerial or social service.

On the intellectual side his was far and away one of the great minds of that era. And he was well aware of it. While he undoubtedly never classified himself as narcissistic one remark alone, to the effect that, "my mind might expand and show out capacity as ample and important as Locke's or Newton's or Witherspoon's," clearly demonstrates his tendency in that direction.

No engraving or painting of Fithian has survived the years, hence his physical characteristics are undeterminable. But it is known that he was hypersensitive and upon correction or reproof would become sullen and low spirited. Like Whitefield, a fellow preacher, he was partly prima donna and highly extrovert when the audience, be it small or large, was with him; but in the absence of such acclaim, he became dejected.

His experiences on the frontier as recorded in his Journal did not all deal with saving souls or with lyric visions of America's future. He was decidedly objective in his point of view; writing of a poor family with whom he was obliged to spend the night, "Fleas biting, bugs crawling,—on a hard board surrounded by a snoring Family."

At Woodstock, Virginia, he relates a case of conjugal delinquency, adding his own observations at the end. "Last Week Something singular befel one of the Inhabitants; Mr.——— An Irishman hired in a Store was taken in an Attempt to spend the Night with a Matron of the Town—Her Husband however by a Stratagem found them in Bed with each other—He entered the Room—The Gallant leaped out from a Window above Stairs quite naked of everything but his Shirt—His Wig, Shoes and Stockings, Hat & Cane he had left without the door to secure them against Surprize—His Breeches, Waistcoat & a Cloak, he left behind—With these the angry Husband heated the Stove for his own Satisfaction—Poor Redress—He ought to have added the Sinning Wife."

Out in the lovely Susquehanna valley near Sunbury, Fithian ruminated on the vast beauties of nature, then turned to the subject of Divine Neatness in Women, to end up with this startling and abrupt dissertation on Wantoness: "But I have never yet met with any Author who has with sufficent *Strength* & *Fullness*, not even Swift himself, express'd himself, in *Words* equal to my *Thoughts* of a SLUT."

The missionary was both ironic and humorous in his report of moral lapses on the part of two church members at Berkeley, Virginia: "—Upon my Word, it is true, one of the Pillars; & the very strongest in the whole Building too, of the Presbyterian Church in Berkeley, most unluckily gave Way this Afternoon & lies upon the Ground—It is nothing in all the World but a Metaphor;—The ruling Elder was *drunk*. (Note, the word "drunk" is in italics). Major Willis has a Mistress. What of that; so has the King of France."

Enroute west for his second tour, Fithian stopped in Salem and left a note for posterity, on the lack of patriotic zeal in the twin town. The subject and the ensuing discussion apparently pleased Fithian's ego, He wrote: "Parson, your most humble Servant, said Lieutenant Nigley (actually Samuel

---

53

Neglee) to me in high good Humour. This Salem, Parson, is but a dull Town. I have been here attempting to raise Recruits these four Days— Four Days & Five Men. This is the 13th day of November, 1775. I have left my Relations, Friends & Broke from inglorious Ease to serve my Country. And you also, Parson, have a few hours ago, left, all, even your dear dear Betsy, tho' so very lately connected with her & are now going on the Service of your God—I think, said the polite Lieutenant, we are both in an honourable Cause, let us then defend it with our Property & Blood, if the Call is so loud."

Outstanding in the masterly attributes of Fithian's mind was his great gift of prophecy. It is safe to say that there were few men in the colonies at that day who could foresee and predict with the accuracy that he did. It is a magnificent tribute to him that every single portion of his prophecy came true. In cold fact every American citizen alive today has seen the accomplished fact of his prediction, one hundred and seventy odd years ago.

The following apostrophe to America was written in his Journal, at Cedar Creek, in the Shenandoah Valley, June 1, 1775:

"The melancholy Anniversary of a tyrannical Manouvre of the infatuated or rather Hell-inspired British Ministry in blocking up the Port of Boston is arrived. —This Day Twelve Month their dangerous & cruel Councels began to be executed.—All along the Bladder has been filling with Venom. Now it is distended with Poison—full, ready to crack, to split with Rage! —Feeble and unavailing efforts! Three Thousand British Forces were sent & are now to be joined by two thousand More, with two hundred horse —Five thousand hireling Regulars at Sixpence Ster; per Day, most of them young & unused to Hardships. Five Thousand hireling Britons against the Millions of America's hardy Sons—The Odds is five thousand against thirty hundred thousand; And all these Myriads fighting for what is dear to them as Life, which they will as soon give up to Power!—

Double fireplace in the Stiles Sheppard House.

Stiles Sheppard House.

Rinehart House.

Interior of Rinehart House.

Table used for making dough in Phelps Rinehart House.

The Dennis House.

"O America! Unwieldy Mass of Earth, pleasant & healthful—Tho' various in thy Climes—Fertile of every Useful Support of Life—On thy Bosom, exuberant of Nourishment have been raised a wise & gigantic People—They are now flourishing in Learning & Arts, & chiefly, at present, urged on by a misjudging Ministry, & preparing with a Confidence of Success to rival the Whole World in Milatary Honour.

"O America! with Reverence I look forward & View Thee in Distinguished Majesty—It is not rash to assert, without the Aid of Prophecy, that thy Commerce & Thy Wealth & Power are Yet to rule the Globe!

"The March of Commerce & Improvement to the westward, is so rapid, that soon, perhaps before the present Century is quite filled up, we shall have Towns overlooking the Banks of the Pacifick Ocean."

In late February of 1776, he returned from his second and last frontier tour. He stayed at Deerfield with his wife who had been residing there for some time past with her sister, Mrs. Enoch Green. There seems to have been no attempt on Fithian's part to establish a home for his bride, although his parents had both died in 1772 and, as the eldest son under the law of primogeniture, he had a large farmhouse at his disposal. The only domestic note that appears at this time is in May, when he went to Philadelphia to purchase "printed cotton" for his wife.

On June 14th, the New Jersey Provincial Congress voted to raise five battalions of militia to serve six months. The two inseparables, Hunter and Fithian, immediately secured commissions as chaplains in this brigade. Fithian was assigned to his fellow townsman, Colonel, later Brigadier General, Silas Newcomb, and Hunter to a North Jersey battalion. Their pay was set at thirty-three-and-a-third dollars a month.

By July 12th, Phillip was in New York, at which point his war diary and the concluding pages of his Journal begin. As the record of a meticulous and honest observer, his accounts of the operations around Manhattan and

---

of the disastrous American defeat in the Battle of Long Island have been much used by later historians.

The love letters of Phillip Vickers Fithian written to his wife, Elizabeth Beatty Fithian, chiefly from the New York area in the summer and early fall of 1776, were compiled and published by the late Frank DeWitt Andrews at Vineland, New Jersey, in 1932. With true Victorian prudery, the compiler apologizes for their publication on the grounds that the letters were "intimate." (Most love letters are.) However, they were fortunately published and a researcher into Fithian's brief but hectic career has reason to be thankful, because they reveal also that the romance was a bit one-sided and that "Laura," like many other women, apparently preferred a home and a husband to a hero and a travelling missionary.

The facts speak sadly for themselves. A three weeks' honeymoon, then off to the frontier to preach. A brief reunion of not over ninety days, then off to the wars as a chaplain. It is eloquent and pathetic that when Fithian lay dying at Harlem Heights, Elizabeth, although sent for by Andrew Hunter and with ample notice, did not attempt the trip.

Quite at random, a dozen excerpts are here quoted in the letters from Phillip to Elizabeth. (Her few letters, three in all, to him have not been preserved.) While Fithian first used the cognomens of "Laura" and "Eliza" in addressing her, he later changed to "Betsy" and also changed his nom-de-plume of "Philander" to P. V. Fithian.

"Be cautious of the evening Damps. Be Home by Sunset or Shortly Thereafter. Do not expose yourself too much; yet exercise about every week."

"Your brother is Hearty but complains of Sore Bones."

"We shall meet again in the World to come."

"Every Default (of not writing to him) I set down as a Breach of what I have a Right to Expect."

"Your interest, my dear Creature, Lies on my soul next to my bleeding Country."

"Why are you formal and cannot Write?"

"Of War, you have had enough in the News; I mean to fill my letters with Love."

"Do not tell me that you are not capable of following the Pattern I set for you. Set down a few Vagrant Thoughts."

"All our Hopes are in Heaven."

"Oh, none but Heaven, you and I can tell the greatness of the Felicity we have possessed together."

"The all important design of Life is to prepare for Eternity."

"Not a Single Rival have you had in my breast since the Hour you consented to be Mine—I have reason to believe the same of you."

His last letter from the camp at Fort Washington, New York City, September 19th, 1776, concludes, "Peace and God's Blessings be with my Betsy, my dear Wife, forever may you be happy." P. V. Fithian."

Returning to his Journal he writes a homely note. During the rather wild retreat of the Americans from Long Island to Upper Manhattan, he lost "a Neat Pewter Porringer & Spoon & a Bottle of Choice Spirits." He was terrified under fire until he saw General George Washington stand calmly on the parapet of Fort Washington, with British bullets whizzing all around him. Then, he writes, he was afraid no longer.

The last entry in his Journal, dated September 22nd, ends on a pessimistic note: "Our Lads grow tired & Begin to count the days of the Service which yet remains." The next day he was stricken with dysentery. At the time, Washington's army lay on Harlem Heights (in modern New York, 125th to 133rd street, west side). There are accounts which say that he died at White Plains but this cannot be true because Washington did not move his forces into Westchester County until October 21st.

There is some comfort in the fact that in his last illness Fithian had three loyal, trusted friends by his side: Doctor Thomas Ewing of Greenwich, then an army surgeon; Chaplain Andrew Hunter, his closest friend; and Chaplain William Hollingshead of Fairfield. On the 28th, Hunter wrote Elizabeth, at Phillip's request. He was quite blunt: "If I were in his situation, should want to see so near a Friend as Wife." But no answer was forthcoming. All three men left accounts in their journals and in letters pertaining to Fithian's last illness. On the early morning of October 8th, Doctor Ewing wrote to Elizabeth at Deerfield that her husband could not survive much longer, that they secured a good feather bed for him to "lye" on, and that he now advised against her coming because it could do no good. At ten, that same morning, Fithian died.

The last word comes from Hunter's Journal dated October 9th: "About 8 O'Clock in the Morning, three of the Ships which lay in the No. River nearly opposite Bloomingdol (Bloomingdale) hoisted their Sails and stood up the River: as soon as they came within reach of our Batteries, we began to play upon them with our Cannon—the first Salute from Fort Constitution, next from Fort Washington, and from 2 Batteries on the Bank of the River—They bore on without firing more than three or four Times, notwithstanding our Chevaux de Frize, and the heaviest fire we could make for an hour and an half—what their Designs are we could not learn—About 10 O'Clock Mr. Fithian was buried—His funeral was attended by several Clergymen and the Officers and Soldiers of Colonel Newcomb's Regt. with as much decency as the nature of the case would allow."

In the final analysis, Fithian was as ardent an American patriot as ever lived; he truly sacrificed home and love for country; he organized an act of rebellious violence against tyranny, which time has softened into mellow patriotism. And he was also the personification of Greenwich, the town which gave him birth.

Chapter Four

OF THE OLD HOUSES OF GREENWICH

Greenwich is forty-five miles southwest from Philadelphia. An antiquarian-traveller who desires historic flavor over the entire, but much longer route, may take the (1682) Kings Highway from Haddonfield or Woodbury to Salem via the (1638) town of Swedesboro. At Salem, on Yorke Street, begins another Kings Highway (1707) to Greenwich. The last road is now commonly called the Hancock's Bridge road. Five miles south of Salem in the hamlet of Hancock's Bridge is the Hancock House, a state museum, in which house an American militia garrison was massacred by the British in 1778. It is trite but true, to say that along this route lies a vast amount of history.

The more direct but much less historic route is via state highways 45 and 46, Camden to Bridgeton. From this latter place it is seven miles to Greenwich.

A tour of the ancient town and its old houses may well begin about three miles to the northwest at a point on the Salem-Greenwich road known as Gum Tree Corner. Here, on the right, facing south, is a huge and very old gum tree which gives its name to the triple crossroads. The road to the extreme left goes to Roadstown, the center one to Head of Greenwich and the road to the right, by devious turns, eventually ends up in the main part of Greenwich. The road from Gum Tree to the Head of Greenwich presents (unusual for southern New Jersey) a slight aspect of hill and dale,

---

of overlooking foliage high above the road, of a mill pond: a most picturesque entry into a picturesque colonial town. The sand hill once covered by a heavy growth of pine, just as one reaches civilization, is called "Mount Gibbon."

Down from Mount Gibbon and across a run known as Pine Mount, the Head of Greenwich suddenly appears: an old yellow frame store; on the left adjoining it, a line of several houses; a dark red brick church set in a wide green lawn bordered by entirely ivy-covered buttonwoods and elms, a modern cemetery behind the church and across the main road; and another, older cemetery whose ancient tombstones are clearly and plainly visible. Pine Mount Run crossed and the Head of Greenwich reached, the Kings Highway divides into a left road to Springtown and Bridgeton, and a right to Stathems Neck. Straight ahead there stretches, lined by venerable shade trees, the ancient "Greate Streete," laid out in 1684, which here begins its two-and-two-tenths miles course to the wharf at Cohansey Creek. At its beginning, it is eighty feet wide, later on it increases to ninety and for its last mile is an even hundred. Along this proud thoroughfare, Fenwick and his executors sold 16-acre town lots.

The Stathems Neck road and the Bridgeton-Springtown road are not exactly opposite. The latter runs dead end into the old cemetery and the first-named road goes off the King's Highway, about thirty yards above the north end of the graveyard. Opposite in the intervening space, on the east side facing the King's road and before the yellow frame store on the corner is reached, are two small houses, the survivors of four which once were joined together and known as the Arcade. Because they were built by a certain Noah Flanigan, the group was once called the Ark.

On the northeast corner where the Bridgeton road joins the Great Street is Clinton Campbell's frame store, which is in two sections. The easterly section was probably built by 1765; the other, by 1810. Advertising signs for popular beverages and the like have quite ruined the colonial exterior aspect, but a single glance either inside or out, is convincing of its great age. How long this property has been a store is anyone's guess, but the best available records attest to the fact that it was such before the revolution. The name attached to this store corner, for decades, was Stathem.

Next on the east is another old residence, a brick house built by Noah Flanigan, also the "creator of Noah's Ark," early in the 19th century. It was long occupied by Doctor Thomas Stathem, and after his death by the late Miss Mary Bacon Watson who wrote much, for local consumption, of the village life. Their combined tenures amounted to almost a century in time. It is now the home of Mr. and Mrs. J. Meade Landis.

There is, in this house, a graceful stairway which is open, "in a well," to the third story. There are also four fireplaces, all of which may still be used, and a great deal of old hardware. Reminiscent of Bordentown, New Jersey, many of whose houses possess fine wrought iron grille work, this house has a similar impressive example on its front porch.

Possibly fifty yards east from the store corner on the north or same side of the Bridgeton road-street, there is an old weather beaten, rather dilapidated frame dwelling. This is the Doctor Samuel Ward house and it was built about 1760. A lean-to portion fell in ruins some years ago, and was torn down. This house was built by Doctor Ward, one of the very first practitioners of medicine in southern New Jersey. His untimely death at the age of 38 in 1774 is noted by Fithian in his Journal, and the tombstone in the old graveyard extolls at some length his virtues.

But the house is much more noted as the residence of Doctor Enoch Fithian who lived to be over a hundred years old (May 1792-November 1892) and is a literary shrine of the highest importance. In this house Doctor Fithian compiled, edited and preserved the priceless Journal of Phillip Vickers Fithian.

Phillip died in 1776. In 1780 his widow married Joel Fithian, a first cousin of the journalist. They had five children: Enoch was one; another, Charles Beatty Fithian, was the great-great-grandfather of the compiler of this book. Enoch was named for Phillip's brother, a cripple, into whose hands the Journal was delivered by Andrew Hunter after Phillip's untimely death. The elder Enoch in later years turned it over to the younger. The Doctor having saved it for approximately eight decades gave it, just before his death, to another relative, Edward W. Hitchcock of Philadelphia, with the stipulation that it be given to Princeton University. In 1900, the first portion was printed by that institution's press.

Doctor Enoch was a lifelong and ardent member of the Presbyterian church, choir leader, elder, etc. On a trip to Boston, he brought back seedlings of the elm trees which now give full shade to the spacious lawn of the church. He wrote a history of the congregation which is an extremely valuable source book.

On May 10, 1892, several hundred people came to Greenwich on the anniversary of the Doctor's one hundredth birthday. Relatives came from such distant points as East Braintree, Massachusetts, and Steubenville, Ohio.

The doctor appeared on the front porch, made a brief address to the friends and relatives as well as to the student body cadet corps of the West Jersey Academy. The corps had marched seven miles to attend the festivities. Very appropriately and effectively the cententarian closed his brief address with these words, "Time has laid its hand upon my heart gently, not smiting, but as a harper lays his open palm upon his harp to deaden its vibrations."

As the cadets drilled to the tune of their band, the Doctor, sitting in a rocker on the front porch kept time to the music by tapping his slippered feet.

The Wood Mansion built in 1795 by Richard Wood. Now the home of the Cumberland County Historical Society.

Fireplace in Wood Mansion.

Colonial bedroom in Wood Mansion.

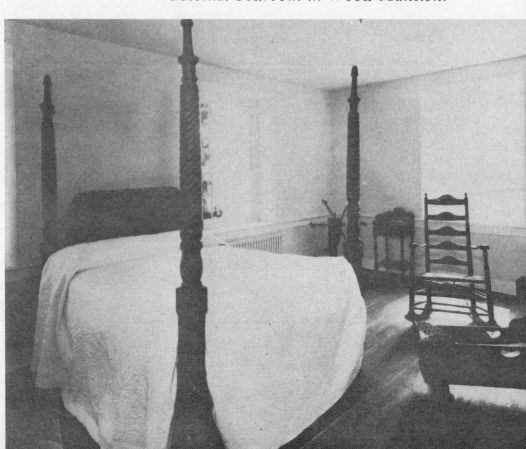

There were of course many speeches, most of them by Presbyterian ministers. Former United States Senator Alexander Gilmore Cattell, a native of Salem, made the pertinent statement that Doctor Enoch had lived under every President of the United States from Washington to Harrison. (Actually he was destined to live long enough to see another man, Grover Cleveland, elected because his death did not occur until mid-November of 1892.) It was also pointed out that he was the oldest living Freemason in the nation, the oldest member of any Presbyterian congregation and the oldest alumnus of the University of Pennsylvania (class of 1817).

A half-century and more has passed since the Ward house was the scene of the centenarian's birthday. A relative-guest on that occasion, now nearing the age of eighty, recalls that her outstanding recollection of that day is the overwhelming fragrance of the lilies of the valley which grew profusely in the doctor's colonial garden.

Mention has been made that the doctor preserved the Journal of his mother's first husband, but a different and near tragic fate almost overtook the love letters of Philander to his Laura. For over a century they had been in the possession of Elizabeth Fithian or of her son, Enoch, who, incidentally never married, and one supposes that there was a certain pride or delicacy about publishing or even mentioning love letters from the dead. When the sale following the doctor's death was held, the late Frank De-Witt Andrews of Vineland, New Jersey, whose wife was Rebecca Graham Ayars of Greenwich, noticed out in the yard a box of books on the top of which was laid a crocheted work bag. Opening the draw strings out of curiosity, Andrews saw therein a packet of letters signed by Phillip Vickers Fithian. Not knowing the full extent of his discovery, he bid the bag and contents in for ten cents. Thus, for a dime he saved the now well-known letters to Laura. Years later, (in 1932), Andrews also had qualms about publishing them, but finally did.

Doctor Fithian's niece, Miss Mary Fithian (who died in 1907), a daughter of Enoch's brother, Charles Beatty, lived with him for many years as a housekeeper. At least two writers made public their indebtedness to her for historic and family information: John Rogers Williams, editor of Princeton's first edition of the Journal; and Everett T. Tomlinson, author of a boy's book on the Tea Burning.

Past the Ward-Fithian house the road leads on to Springtown, a Negro settlement, which may have derived its name from the fact that its first Negro settlers were literally "sprung" from slavery thanks to the medium of the Underground Railroad. Greenwich Quakers were instrumental in maintaining a station or haven of escape for fugitive slaves from the south. The commonly accepted derivation of the name comes from the numerous springs at this place.

Greenwich was an important junction on the Underground since it was the first stopping place of refuge on the eastern side of Delaware Bay from the Delmarva peninsula, which was one of the hardest places for a fugitive slave to pass, as the stories of Patty Cannon, notorious slave stealer, told in George Alfred Townsend's *Entailed Hat,* will attest.

A minister named Thomas Clement Oliver at Salem was the director of this south Jersey section of the Underground, in and around Greenwich. In those days, 1820 to 1860, many free Negroes volunteered to act as guides from Delaware across the Bay to Cohansey. One combined guide-reception committee was a Negro woman named Harriet Tubman who fed the colored babies on paregoric and carried them in small wicker baskets like puppies. Also active at Greenwich was John Mason, another free man who boasted that he had aided 1,800 Negroes to freedom via the Underground Railroad at Greenwich. This compiler knows of one house at Salem, from whence the route lay on to Swedesboro, which was equipped with a dungeon in the cellar for hiding fugitive slaves as they passed through that town on their way north. This is the Morris Hancock house built in 1816 at 314 East Broadway and known familiarly as the Owen Jones-Clayton residence. This built-in wooden dungeon was opened by a sliding secret door; there were three casks therein for the fugitive Negroes to sit on while waiting for the cover of darkness to proceed. However, some few years ago, in placing a new furnace in the cellar this old hiding place was torn out.

The south side of the Springtown road is not built up as is the north side. Opposite the Ward house is the "new" cemetery of the Presbyterian church, so-called to differentiate it from the older one on the west side of the great street. In front of the new graveyard is the dark red brick Presbyterian church.

This church was built in 1835 and replaced the 1735 one which stood directly opposite in the middle of the ancient burying ground. Over a century old, it is an excellent example of solid plain style and expert workmanship.

About where this church stands, George Whitefield, finding the edifice of that day (1740) too small to hold his audience estimated at 3,000 people, preached in the open air.

After approximately a century of use, the old church became so dilapidated that it was torn down and the present one erected across the Great Street to the east. Doctor Fithian left a description of the early church. It was of brick, 34 by 44 feet, two stories high, but oddly enough the galleries were reached by outside stairs. Downstairs, pews lined the walls and the rougher, unfinished benches were placed in the center. The pride of the church was its pulpit which had been made in Boston. It was hexagonal in shape, made of black walnut wood, with sounding boards ornamented in different colored woods, and overhead in the canopy above the pulpit was a star ornament radiating from a circle near the center.

The old cemetery is not free from long, eulogistic, religious epitaphs, nor from some humorous ones as well. And as befitted a prosperous community, its wealth was exhibited in the expenditure for memorials to the dead. In most rural sections the dead were buried on the farm, sometimes with monuments, more often without. Here, at Greenwich, are large, expensive, flat and raised sepulchre curved tombstones, shafts, tablets and the like. Nor was expense spared in stone cutting. Life histories, poetry, hymns, and long eulogies are given in the cold stone on most of the monuments. An excellent example is that of Phoebe Bloomfield.

"A Memorial of Phoebe Bloomfield. Daughter of Jonathan Holmes Esq. In June 1766 she married Doctor Ward of Greenwich and survived her husband. Was again married, Dr. Bloomfield of Woodbridge in 1775, whom she survived and departed this life after a tedious and severe illness on the 29th of August, 1820 in the 72nd year of her age. She was a member of the Presbyterian church upwards of twelve years and was esteemed by all her connections and acquaintances."

"Our age to seventy years is set,
How short the time; how frail the state,
And if to eighty we arrive
We'd rather sigh and groan than live."

Incidentally the lady was the step-mother of Joseph Bloomfield, the fourth governer of New Jersey.

Close by is her first husband's grave, also a massive affair. "Memorial of Samuel Ward who departed this life, Feb. 27, 1774 in the 38th year of his age. This inscription is a small tribute to the memory of the once humane, generous and just, the uniform friend, the tender husband, the assiduous and skillful physician, the Lover of his Country and a Real Christian. The last end of the good man in peace."

Another example of the piety as preserved by the stone cutter, is the tablet for Esther Maskell: "In memory of Esther Maskell, relict of Thomas Maskell, Esq. dec'd, who died September 11, 1805 in the 58th year of her age. She was an affectionate and condescending wife, a tender and indulgent parent and a bright pattern of domestic religion, was attendant and devout and died in the Faith of Jesus Christ and lively hope of Redemption through his Blood.

"Let surviving friends be solicitous in imitating her virtues and follow her footsteps as she followed Christ and did good and to improve their bereavement by diligent preparations for meeting her in a future state."

> *"Hear what the world from Heaven declares,*
> *To those in Christ who die*
> *Released from all the earthly cares*
> *They reign with him on high."*

A somewhat enigmatic inscription is on the tomb of Samuel M. Dowdrey, M. D. 1834-1861—"I was dumb—I opened not my mouth because thou didst it."

And Sallie J. Hawkins, who died June 17, 1863, left this injunction: "Husband weep not for me, Go home dry up your tears."

There are many small flags waving in the small cemetery, practically every one marking the grave of a Revolutionary veteran. Five tea burners are buried here: Thomas Ewing, Enos Ewing, James Hunt, Joel Miller and Joel Fithian. Next to Joel Fithian lies his wife, Elizabeth Beatty-Fithian-Fithian, the "Laura" of so long ago.

And of these last two graves there comes a final note from Bessie Ayars Andrews, the historian of Greenwich. On an evening in the year 1865, she and her brother passing the yard at sundown on their way home, heard a clear firm strong voice singing, "There is a land of pure delight where saints immortal reign." Startled, they stood transfixed, to behold Doctor Fithian, his white hair visible in the failing light, standing by the tomb of his parents and singing to the end the stanzas of the ancient hymn.

The western boundary of the burying ground is Pine Mount Run, which after the Kings Highway has crossed it, north to south, abruptly turns west at the back of the cemetery. Coursing west, then south, for about two miles through Bacon's Neck it joins the Cohansey. The stream's change of course at this point was responsible for the building of the church, for in those days, farmers who rode miles to religious services needed watering places for their horses. Here was a pleasant meadow, here a fresh pure stream, therefore the church. In some cases, of course, navigable streams were responsible for the location of the houses, churches and even towns but Pine Mount Run was too small to fill that category.

After modern literature with its overdose of psychiatric novels of murders, conjugal infidelity and the like, it is refreshing, without being stilted or editorial, to read a book like Bessie Ayers Andrews', *Historical Sketches of Greenwich in old Cohansey.* The peace, the charm, the rural simplicity of another age, and one that still lives in Greenwich, come out in full force from her little book. Of Pine Mount Run, which was near her home, she writes: "Our favorite place was near the old bridge where the willow boughs swayed in the soft western wind and in the topmost branches, the cardinal bird in his brilliant plumage trilled his melodious song."

In the immediate vicinity of the Run, east from the King's Road, once stood a fulling mill, now vanished save for a few rotted door sills, where the home spun bedding and clothing were dressed by use of pestles or stamps which beat the material to a close or compact mass after it was first cleansed.

74

Close to a mile north of Pine Mount Run and at this point flowing in the same direction, is a run retaining the delightful Indian name of Macanippuck. Here, near the King's Road to Salem was a grist mill, erected by the Gibbons before 1700. According to Historian Robert Gibbon Johnson, it was at first a wind mill, then later changed over to water power. This mill has quite vanished.

Romantically, Mrs. Andrews recalls the grist mill: "At the old mill one lovely spring morning, a beautiful maiden stood in the doorway waiting her turn. . . . The birds on the willow branches were carrolling their songs of gladness when a youth approached, saw the young maiden, fell in love with her, right then and there, proposed and was accepted. . . . soon afterwards married her." She names the young and impetuous lover as Thomas Maskell of Vauxhall Gardens.

Of Mount Gibbon, above the run: "Here we found the pink and white trailing arbutus in the springtime, then as the seasons progressed, the pink mocassin shoe and the dog-toothed violets, the wild honey suckle, the stately laurel with its pinkish white cup like blooms, the magnolia with its aromatic whiff of sweet perfume above our heads, the modest pipsissaway opening snowy petals at our feet, and finally as the days grew shorter and colder there appeared the holly for Christmas time, flowering with its red hard beads against the white background of snow."

This part of Greenwich has had several names. Long and properly known as the Head of Greenwich because "Ye Greate Streete" begins there, it has also been called North Greenwich. And, many decades ago, it was decided to establish a post office there, making a separate town of it, since it was two miles to the main portion of Greenwich. The government asked for a name and the citizens chose "Othello." The post office named by Shakespearean lovers of long ago is gone and today few, if any, refer to it as Othello although some road maps carry that name as well as North Greenwich.

There is a frame dwelling house on the right, or west, side just below the graveyard which is more interesting for what it was rather than what it is now. Quakers, Baptists, Presbyterians and Episcopalians all had and maintained churches up to the revolution. The latter congregation (Saint Stephens) died out about that period and no new sects have since been successful in establishing themselves in Greenwich. However in 1790, the Methodists, then beginning to flourish in the new republic, attempted to establish a church at the Head of Greenwich. They erected a frame structure on the south side of Mount Gibbon near Pine Mount Run. Like its near neighbor, the old brick Presbyterian church, it had outside staircases leading to the galleries. The Methodists could not compete and soon died out.

About 1827 the abandoned church was bought by the Hicksite Quakers. The necessity of the purchase was occasioned by the split over fundamentalism within the Society of Friends over the question of the Divinity. The liberal side was called Hicksites after their leader, Elias Hicks. The conservative group was known as Orthodox. The latter faction, by a famous and bitter law suit, retained practically all the meeting houses in New Jersey, thus causing the Hicksite faction to buy or build. (At the twin town of Salem the reverse was true. Here the Hicksites retained the 1772 meeting house and the Orthodox was forced to build.)

At Greenwich the Orthodox retained the massive 1771 edifice near Cohansey wharf, while the Hicksites acquired the old frame Methodist church and moved it from Mount Gibbon, about a furlong south, to the east side of the Great Street. The first floor was used for meetings; the second for a school. In 1857, the Quakers built their present brick meeting house and moved the church that had done duty for two different faiths back towards the Head of Greenwich, thus ending its hegira by leaving it on the west side of the street where it was transformed into a dwelling house.

The Gibbon House with red and blue Flemish Bond Brick. The date of erection (1730) is on the plaque at the peak.

House at Sheppard's Mills.

Detail of Bull's-Eye doorway in
Sheppard-Holmes House.

Interior Reeve Sheppard House.

Exterior Gabriel Davis House.

The next house south, on the same side, is another frame dwelling more interesting because of its one time owner than for any other reason. In 1800, when the Negro revolt broke out against French rule in Haiti, a young man named Jean Jacques Coner Deroi escaped from the holocaust and embarked on a boat which docked at Greenwich. Satisfied, he settled in this, the very first place he came to. Grateful for this haven in a free land, Deroi changed his name to William Williams, choosing the name of a Connecticut signer of the Declaration of Independence.

On the east side of the Great Street, nearly opposite the Deroi-Williams house is a large frame house known as the Test property. This house has a plain yet attractive fanlight over the front door. A little further south and there appears the red brick meeting house of the Hicksite Quakers which is still in use. A white marble plate on the gable attests to its date—1857.

The west side presents, about eighty yards from the cemetery, the first brick dwelling which is flush on the Great Street. This is the Ewing house built in 1765 by Samuel Ewing, now owned and occupied by Mary Bacon Gallagher and her husband, George. Stucco covers the ancient brick work but ivy has partially covered the stucco. The house is in two sections: the upright, or two stories and an attic; and the lower portion, commonly called a "dropped wing." Mrs. Gallagher has furnished the house with heirlooms of her family, the Bacons, one of the first settlers in Greenwich. The house is immaculate, both interior and exterior, and it is truly one of the antique landmarks of the town.

Past the Friend's Meeting house and a dead end Bridgeton road crossing, out in the open country now, with the overhanging, overlapping foliage gone, temporarily, from the Great Street, the road turns sharply to the right and widens out from eighty feet to ninety. In the angle on the west side is a brownstone building with white shutters, a story and a half in height, built in 1811 and successively used as a militia headquarters, school house, polling booth, undertaker's establishment and now as an art museum. The wealth of subject matter in Greenwich has not gone unnoticed by artists. Several reside in the town; and their county association meets monthly here to exhibit their individual works.

South of the brownstone and opposite, across the Great Street, since it here changes its direction to east-west, is a vacant field known as the "Town Place." It was left by Zachariah Barrow in his will (1725) "for the use of a free school for the poor children of Greenwich forever," an eleemosynary grant that was never fulfilled. A field it was then, and a field it is now. Barrow was land-rich but personal property-poor. However, his good intent and the pathos back of his motive in so deeding the land by will, appears clearly in the inventory of his estate filed at the Secretary of State's office in Trenton. His possessions were meagre. To quote the schedule: "one bed, two sheets, two pillow cases, one table and ONE BOOK."

A few rods further west on the same, or south side, of the Great Street is the low walled enclosure, green "carpeted," well trimmed, and neatly kept burial ground of the Society of Friends. There is a story of an old lady from Indiana visiting in Greenwich, who when she saw this graveyard, insisted that she be buried there, because, "it looks so peaceful." Small headstones or plain grave markers adorn a few graves; the vast majority of the dead lie unmarked and unknown. For ornamentation, even after death, was frowned upon by the early Quakers, who literally believed in "ashes to ashes," and "dust to dust," and consequently would not countenance any marble memorials for the departed. A little over a century ago agitation was started to at least remember the person who was buried there, by a small marker giving the name and dates. That custom prevails today.

Past the frame school house, opposite the Friend's Burying Ground, the Great Street turns and bends for the last time, assuming here a width of an even hundred feet which it maintains to its end at the creek a mile away. The street also changes direction from east-west to north-south again, its direction as it leaves the King's Highway at its beginning point at the head of Greenwich. Set in the right angle of the road at this final bend is a rather severe-looking brick house, stuccoed over, built in the familiar upright and dropped wing portions. The fanlight over the front door is an exceedingly fine piece of workmanship. This is the Charles Beatty Fithian house. It was built in 1800 by Enos Ewing, one of the tea burners, whose daughter married Fithian.

South on the last stretch of the Great Street, there is open country on either side, then a group of nondescript houses, the Baptist church on the left, a canning factory on the right (one of the town's two contributions to industry) and across the street is a cinder blackened gash, the last reminder of the once proud New Jersey Central Railroad which ran from Jersey City to Bayside. At this point on the right stood the yellow-painted Greenwich railroad station. Ironically enough, the railroad which changed some towns completely had no perceptible effect on Greenwich. It came in 1870, it went in 1935, a life span of about one-fourth that of the town.

Before you now, stretching to the Cohansey, lies untouched, unrestored, pristine, original colonial Greenwich. At the old railroad crossing one may stand and look down that wide green canopied vista of "Ye Greate Streete" and recall some anonymous lines:

> "Mix their boughs and interlace,
> In a slumbrous fond embrace
> Where the one great street runs down
> To the wharf at Greenwich Town."

The fieldstone tavern, once the court house of Cumberland County, was built about 1730. It was not the first tavern in Greenwich; as early as 1696 Jeremiah Bacon, describing himself as "innkeeper," bought a sixteen-acre town lot. At historic random the Salem county court granted licenses at Greenwich to Jacob Ware, 1728 to 1742, William Watson, 1733 to 1742, James Carruthers, 1737-1739, John Foster, 1737, Fitz Randolph, 1739, and John Butler, 1741-1742. Of all these hostelries, only two are now traceable: the stone tavern and the Ewing-Bacon-Gallagher house at the Head of Greenwich.

In 1733, agitation was started in the provincial legislature to form a new county out of the southern part of Salem, but the move failed. In 1747, renewed agitation was successful and a new county was created on January 19th, 1747-8 (old style). About four hundred thousand acres were taken from Salem to constitute the new county, named Cumberland in honor of the King's brother, the Duke of Cumberland.

The county seat was placed at Greenwich and in this old tavern the first courts of the new shire were held on May 10-11th, 1748. However, the town was not new to courts; for approximately twenty years before that time travelling sessions of the Salem County courts were held alternately in the tavern and in the Presbyterian Meeting House. This was due to the great distance (for those times) between Salem and Greenwich.

For eleven months of the year 1748, Greenwich enjoyed being the shire town of Cumberland County. Then, by act of the legislature, an election was held to determine the permanent county seat. The Greenwichites apparently went to sleep at election time for the result showed a majority for Cohansie Bridge. Therefore, in December, the courts held their fourth and last session in the old tavern then moved to Bridgeton. The original officials of Cumberland County were Richard Wood, John Brick and John Remington, judges, Ananias Sayre, sheriff, and Elias Cotting, clerk.

The last session of the court did not pass without excitement. The local citizens, enraged at the success of the Cohansie Bridge folks who had, they claimed, "stolen the election, and the court house," went into the tap-room-court-room, kicked the chairs to pieces, smashed all the bar-room s glassware against the wall and started a free-for-all riot. This mob action was particularly hard on the "Mine Host" of that day, who not only lost the rent for the court house but his stock in trade as well. He probably thought, and bitterly, that his irate fellow townsmen could have done just as well, if not better, by a little trespass on the case and wilful damage at any given hostelry in Cohansie Bridge.

However, there is little doubt but what this move saved for posterity the colonial appearance and charm of the town. A county seat cannot re-sist progress. Save for a few old houses, Bridgeton has entirely lost any re-semblance to a colonial town. It is the same with most county seats in the state.

Its brief session as a hall of justice over, the tavern continued in its origin-al purpose for another century, until about the time of the Civil War when it closed its bar and its doors as a tavern and became a residence. (There were other taprooms in Greenwich until the arrival of the Prohibition Amendment in 1920; since that time the town and the township have both been dry.)

The stone tavern is now occupied by Mr. and Mrs. Alexander Lee. Mr. Lee is an artist whose water colors of Greenwich adorn the same walls at which, two centuries ago, infuriated Greenwichites hurled glasses in the court house riot.

The tavern is two-and-a-half stories high, built of fieldstone through-out and has a brick flooring in the basement.

Because of meticulous regard in the regulations imposed by the Salem County court in dispensing liquor licenses prior to 1748, the prices and ingredients of the various drinks have been preserved, without the medium of a bartender's guide. As of 1729, a catalogue of prices that the taverns could charge was as follows:

A rub of punch made with double re popular drinks, which consisted of rum—9 d. (pence).
A rub of punch made with single refined sugar and one-and-a-half gills of rum—8 d.
A rub made of Muscovado sugar and one-and-a-half gills of rum—7 d.
A quart of flip made of a pint of rum—9 d.
A pint of wine—1 shilling.
A gill of rum—3 d.
A quart of strong beer—4 d.
A gill of brandy or cordial—6 d.
A quart of metheglin—9 d.
A quart of cider royal—8 d.
A quart of cider—4 d.

Shilling about 24 cents today.
Pence equal to 2 cents.

And of recipes:
Punch was sweetened liquor prepared with many flavors, and was served in large bowls, some of which are still preserved by the residents of the village. Toddy was made of sweetened liquors and hot water and was served in large tumblers.
The ingredients of flip were home-brewed ale, sugar, and jamaica rum. It was usually heated with an iron stick, called a loggerhead, which was placed in the live coals, until it became red hot, then thrust into the mixture, making it boil and seethe, and giving it a burnt, bitter taste, which was considered palatable; then a mug of flip was ready for the thirsty

traveller or flip lover. It was usually served in a pewter mug. Metheglin was another of those old time popular drinks, which consisted of rum, sugar and honey.

Across the Great Street from the tavern is the magnificent Wood Mansion built in 1795 by Richard Wood. For years it was the summer home of his son, Doctor George Bacon Wood, one of the great names in American medical history. It is now leased by the Cumberland County Historical Society as a museum. The house is built of brick with two sections, the upright and the "dropped wing." The main doorway is a thing of beauty with its four-panel-divisioned fanlight and the huge silver knocker. Trellises keep the climbing and ubiquitous ivy in place.

The mansion's chief glory was its garden. An iron fence surrounded it. The garden gate still bears a name plate, "Dr. George B. Wood." Here boxbushes and hollyhocks which line the walks through which a flock of peacocks once majestically strutted erect with their brilliant many-hued plumage are still seen. (The compiler has a memento from this garden: to-wit, a plume of a peacock.)

The son of the builder, George Bacon Wood, was born in this mansion on March 13, 1797. He graduated from the college of the University of Pennsylvania in the class of 1815 and from the school of medicine in 1818. He was professor of chemistry at the Philadelphia College of Pharmacy for nine years, and of materia medica there and at the University of Pennsylvania for a total of nineteen years. In 1865 he endowed an auxiliary chair on the theory and practice of medicine at the University. Wood was one of the foremost medical writers of his day. In 1847 he wrote, *Treatise on the Practice of Medicine,* in 1836, *Therapeutics and Pharmacology,* and in 1833, with Franklin Bache, M.D., he compiled, *The Dispensatory of the United States,* which volume by 1894 had run into its 17th edition. Wood died in Philadelphia on March 30th, 1879.

Bacon's Neck Street begins alongside the Wood mansion. Across it is the old frame Richard Wood store, which dates back as a retail establishment to at least 1795, and perhaps earlier. It is certainly one of the oldest retail stores in America, boasting a continuous existence for a century and a half. Beginning in about 1685, fairs were conducted semi-annually in Greenwich, in April and October. In 1765 retailers objected to the commercial inroads of travelling peddlars and the fairs were abolished. Legend has it that Richard Wood, the store keeper, was largely instrumental in abolishing the fairs so that his emporium would suffer no loss in trade. Whatever date the store was built, its hardware alone testifies to great age. The lock on the front door is massive, the key equals in size the famous Bastille key in Paris. For years this grocery store was operated by the late Mrs. Emily Lawrence, a direct descendant of Joel and Elizabeth Fithian. It is now operated by Joseph Newkirk.

The illustrations show more vividly than can be described the exquisite street scene south from this point. On the left standing alone, is the Gibbon mansion (1730). On the right is a series of houses, each of which is well over a century old. The oldest is the "hip-roofed" house erected by Richard Wood about 1760. The hip-roofed is a style of colonial architecture now obsolete. It was so named because of its resemblance to a person's hips. About a century ago there lived in this house a man named May. He was a champion pedestrian. He walked to work to Bridgeton (seven miles one way) every day but Sunday and often on Sundays would walk to Philadelphia (45 miles) for relaxation.

Next door but one to the Wood hip-roofed house in a northerly direction is the residence of Mr. and Mrs. Charles Landis, both well known artists.

The Gibbon house on the east side was erected in 1730, a white plaque high on the south gable giving that date. It was built by Nicholas Gibbon

Howell House where Tea Burners met.

Charles Beatty Fithian House. Erected 1800.

who resided there for ten years and then moved to Salem. Nicholas and his brother, Leonard, received as a gift a large tract of land at "Cohansie" from Francis Gibbon in England, who, in turn had received it from a New York cousin, Edmund, who had taken the land in payment for a debt. Francis Gibbon stipulated that the brothers must settle on the land. This they did in the early days of the town and almost single-handedly built Greenwich. The grist mill, the fulling mill, Mount Gibbon, the defunct Saint Stephens church, their own house and others, all recall their vigorous activity. Ships owned by them carried in and out of Greenwich three-fourths of the towns early imports and exports. Nicholas Gibbon was the grandfather of Colonel Robert Gibbon Johnson, the first historian of Salem County and the man who defied sudden death by publicly eating a tomato or "love apple" on the steps of the Salem Court House in 1820. In those days the tomato was thought to be a poisonous fruit. Johnson, who owned half of Salem, named one of the streets he set off for building lots, Gibbon Street, in honor of his grandfather.

The Gibbon house is a splendid example of Flemish bond brick work with its alternate red and blue-header-stretcher brick. The side walls are unadorned save for the white marble plaque bearing the date. The interior of the Gibbon house has not been changed. The spaciousness of the mansion is apparent upon entering the broad hall with the stairway leading upwards. On either side of the entrance are parlors: the right one contains two large corner cupboards, arched over the glass doors, with "butterfly" or indented shelving; the left parlor leads, down three steps, into the kitchen or living room. Here there is a fireplace so huge that it takes away one's breath. This room was not only kitchen and living room, but it was a factory as well. Here, the women-folk spun and wove cloth, dyed it, carded it, sewed, knit, made candles, soap and all other necessities of life. The word, "homespun," describes the gigantic Gibbon living room.

Colonial Bostonians, suffering from lack of food when that port was closed by the British government in 1774, had good reason to be grateful to a man born in this house. He was Grant Gibbon (1734-1776), son of Nicholas, who was chairman of a meeting at Salem which raised and sent to Boston one hundred and fifty-seven pounds sterling for the distressed inhabitants.

An excellent colonial description of the Gibbon house may be found in the *Pennsylvania Gazette* for March 25th, 1759, in which it was advertised for sale:

To Be Sold

A House and lot in the town of Greenwich, in the County of Cumberland, West New Jersey. The house is of brick, large and well built, two stories high, with a large kitchen. It is conveniently situated for a store, also sixteen acres of woodland and two acres and a half of meadow, within three quarters of a mile of the same.

For title and terms apply to the subscribers, in the town of Salem.

GRANT GIBBON

Returning to the west side of the Great Street we find the Daniels house, which has on its rainspout the date—1734. This house has long been known as the Mary W. Bacon house. It is built partly of frame and partly of brick. The north side is definitely the oldest. This house is said to contain a ghost; one of the few in this conservative Quaker town.

In the years before the Revolution, when Spain, France and England were constantly warring with each other, inland waters like the Cohansey, and the Delaware River and Bay knew countless privateers (government licensed pirates). It is a matter of record that a Spanish privateer, a frigate named the La Fortune, out of Havana, Cuba, made a raid on New Castle, Delaware, in May of 1748. The Spaniard attempted another raid on the Jersey side near Salem the following day but was repulsed. However, La Fortune captured a British ship in the river and kindly enough, instead of compelling the prisoners to walk the plank, in keeping with the prevailing custom, turned the twenty-seven members of the crew loose in small boats. The lucky British tars then rowed to Greenwich.

Besides the "licensed" pirates or privateers, there were many who were not so licensed and who also lived by robbery on the seas. Blackbeard (or Teach), Captain Kidd, Worley, Stede Bonnet, to mention only four notorious English-American pirates, knew the Delaware and its tributaries well. Worley, for example, began his career of piratical crime off New Castle.

There were many minor pirates just as many years later there were minor bootleggers on the same waters. Nearness to the Cohansey, and the bay and river was enough temptation for some people who hailed from the Greenwich section to become pirates and prey on the rich shipping that came and went on these waters. Nor was it difficult to slip away from the scene of their naval crime and "to get home," in short order. There was a pirate named, "John," whose last name has mercifully not survived the years. "John" double-crossed his partners-in-crime and "informed." They caught up with him in the attic of his own house (the Daniels), so the yarn goes, and disposed of him by trussing him up in chains, thus leaving him to rot.

On dark, windy nights persons passing the Daniels house have "heard" the rattling, clanking sounds of Pirate "John's" chains as he sought to free himself. This legend was used with telling effect in the late Everett Titsworth Tomlinson's book, a juvenile entitled, *The Campfire of Mad Anthony*, which deals with the Greenwich Tea Party. Tomlinson was a native of nearby Seventh Day Baptist Shiloh; his son Everett, Junior, now owns the Gibbon house.

93

Opposite the Daniel or pirate house, is one of the masterpieces of colonial Greenwich. It is a frame structure known as the Sheppard-Doctor Holmes house (now owned and occupied by Mr. and Mrs. Frank Bonham) and was built prior to 1775, the exact date of erection being unknown. It is popularly known as the Bull's-Eye house because its handsome main doorway is beautifully embellished by four immense green glass "bull's eyes." Considering the scarcity of "optical" glass in the colonies, some unknown did a masterly job. It would seem that they were made to resemble a human eye, but because they were so huge they have been called differently. Bottle-green glass is the predominant color, the iris being a lighter shade than the ring enclosing it from the conjunctiva. The pupil is a darker green, almost a blue, with a surrounding lighter green ring.

Even without the glass ornamentation, the doorway itself is a thing of beauty with its fluted indented markings and severely classic lines. The Bonhams deserve to be called "blessed" as antiquarian restorers, for recently they removed a hideous piazza which for some decades past had hidden the glass eyes from public view. Formerly only by stepping up on the porch could one see the ornaments; now they and the doorway are plainly visible from the street. In the front parlor of the house is a boarded-up fireplace with the same fine indented handwork on the mantel above it as is patent on the front doorway.

Miss Anne Bradway Sheppard of Salem, whose father, Joseph W. Sheppard, was a native of Greenwich, has contributed the following as a personal reminiscence of the house: "In its hey-dey, painted white, facing directly upon the Great Street, it had a beautiful box bush hedge across the front of the flight of steps which one ascended to the doorway. Over the door are the four convex glass bull's-eyes. In the garden at the back were fine old trees and flowering shrubs. Upon entering the house there was a hall with a parlor on one side, the north, while low steps led down to a sitting room, out of which opened a conservatory containing palms, banana trees and other exotic plants. . . . Two elderly ladies shared the home with a village physician, Doctor Ephriam Holmes, a tall slender man who thoroughly enjoyed entertaining guests by playing upon his flute. . . . The mellow atmosphere of the house carried its own air of aristocracy which has lingered in the memory like the fragrance of old lavender. . . ."

Nearly a furlong on the left or east side of the Great Street, south from the Bull's-Eye house, is the dead end of the last of the three roads which end in the street coming from Bridgeton. On the southeast corner are a grocery store and the village post office. The postmaster is Wilbert Arnold, appointed in 1943; prior to him the postmistress for 27 years was appropriately enough a Fithian, Miss Hannah, now retired.

Across the street, facing the Bridgeton road, is a solid, substantial, early American brick dwelling, the home of the Ewings. It was built in 1834 by James Josiah Ewing, a grandson of one of the tea burners. The Ewing house intentionally blocks the road. Prior to 1834 the freeholders of Cumberland County desired to extend this road across the Great Street out through Bacon's Neck, west and south to the lower wharf on the Cohansey now called Greenwich Piers. Mr. Ewing did not relish the prospect of his farmland being cut in half by a road so he hastily had a cellar dug, thus effectively barricading both the proposed road and the plans of the freeholders. Satisfied by this maneuver, he did not attempt to build the house until about eight years later. In the early summer of 1834 it was so cold in late June that the mortar froze and workmen had to quit, gathering around the nearby blacksmith shop's forge to keep warm. (Exactly sixty years before, Phillip Vickers Fithian had recorded a snow storm, and ice in the creek in late May.)

The Ewing family, early settlers in Greenwich, have contributed some great names to the history of both the state and the nation: among them were Thomas Ewing, tea burner, doctor, surgeon in the continental line and in the Navy as well, veteran of Long Island, Harlem Heights, White Plains, Trenton, finally a member of the Legislature of New Jersey; James Ewing, his brother, also a tea burner, legislator, Mayor of Trenton, New Jersey, and author of a revised means of spelling on which subject he published a work entitled *A Columbian Pamphlet,* in 1798; Charles, son of James, Chief Justice of New Jersey from 1824 to 1832; still another Ewing, Thomas, was a United States Senator from Ohio and Secretary of the Treasury under Presidents Harrison and Tyler. The daughter of this Ewing married General William Tecumseh Sherman of Civil War fame who is well remembered for having remarked that "War is Hell."

The Ewing line still carries on in Greenwich. In 1940 the late Charles, then ninety, wrote an interesting letter to the author, succinctly outlining the history of his 1834 house and briefly sketching his family. Excerpts from that letter follow:

Greenwich, June 15, 1940

"Friend Sickler,
In reply to your letter of the 14th will say. The house you speak of "my Homestead" was built in 1834 making its age this year 106. It was built by my father, is a brick mansion, built of brick from "Crum Creek," which is a small creek a short distance above Chester and not of imported brick as was believed by some of the residents of G-. The Ground is on the part of the farm inherited by my great grandfather Thomas Ewing, whom his wife, Sarah Fithian gave him a deed for at her death, as to be inherited by their son, William Bradford Ewing. From this inheritance it came duly to my father James Josiah Ewing. The house was well built and is in good condition today. It is furnished with a lot of antique furniture antedating the Revolution; chairs once belonging

to a relative named Patterson, the first superintendent of the United States Mint in Philadelphia who was so set up by his position, that he cared little or nothing for his furniture but bundled it off to auction. My grandfather promptly bought at auction & I got by inheritance, seven fine chairs, two steel engravings and a lot of deeds. As all lots along Great Street were sold in 16 acre lots, the only way those wily old fellows had to get property in town lots, farms etc. was to get others to buy these lots and so get the land they wanted; what I now possess is a farm lying back of the Great Street. This house was built by a mason-contractor named Randolph. It is a double house, the hall running directly through the center with rooms on either side. The doors are what are known as "Christian," which was a great puzzle to me, until a lady antique dealer gave me the explanation. The way they are panelled made a cross on the upper part. It was a marvel to me as I never heard of a door being "religious" before. There are eight such, in the front of the house.

The back part once the kitchen, now the dining room, has doors that are more modern, in one way or another. The number of antiques has been increased a great deal. There is a High Boy once owned by my great grandfather, a number of tables, some rush bottom chairs, a large sideboard, some samplers, and many more of the same which were allowed to go to pieces, when they were not considered antiques.

There is also a tall clock given to my father and a small mantel wooden works once owned by my niece. In the back of the house there is an oven attached where my mother used to bake for a big family of nine children; seven of us, boys, with the appetites of a steam saw mill. That the house is well built is told by the fact that the front banisters are still in elegant order despite the hard usage of four generations sliding down them. They never even "squeak" when I use them and

I am now over 90 years of age and certainly require their help in going up and down stairs.

I am too old to travel much but stay home mostly, repenting of my past sins and wondering when to look for death as people do not tarry long after four score years and ten. I live with my nephew, Robert P. Ewing, his wife, Grace, their three children and his Daddie now aged 83 at my 90th birthday. On that occasion I had a gang of over sixty relatives and friends but I survived it. There were two, aged 90, two aged 87, two 88, one 85 and one 83. Don't you wonder I lived through it?

 Respectfully Yours,
   Chas. Ewing"

The Bond or Laning house is south past the post office, on the east side of the street. High steps lead to the front door; below are the windows of a ground basement. The roof is long and sloping, one of the few in Fenwick's colony that suggests the Dutch motif; it is all the more unusual since the house was built by the Gibbon brothers in 1725 as a rectory for Saint Stephens Episcopal Church. Despite its great age, the house is still in good condition.

At the turn of the eighteenth century the house was occupied by Doctor Levi Bond. The medico was of tall, spare stature, wore short clothes and exceedingly high boots, all of which gave him an eccentric appearance. Holding peculiar religious views, all his own, he never attended a church. He regarded Saturday as Sunday and refused to do a tap of work on that day, sick patients or no sick patients, but instead withdrew behind the closed and barred shutters of the house for prayer and meditation.

The doctor was nothing if not methodical and to the point. Secretly admiring a young lady of Greenwich and without paying her the slight-

Birthplace and home of Phillip Vickers Fithian. Here the Tea Burners dressed as "Indians" on the night of December 22nd, 1774.

Daniels or Pirate House, built in 1734. The date is visible on the rainspout.

est courtship, he walked into her house and said to her, "Will you marry me?" Just as abruptly, she said, "No," and walked out of the room, leaving her quickly rejected suitor to follow her. Yet old Doctor Bond did rather well for he had three wives and outlived them all. He moved west, died at Roseburg, Indiana, at the age of ninety-three. His obituary describes him "as a shock of corn fully ripe for the Harvest of God."

A frame house stands just south of the Bond dwelling, separated by a modern house and an overgrown weed-filled lot. This lot was the site of the Saint Stephens Episcopal Church. Known as the Judy Husted house, it is supposed to have been the repository of the tea during its brief sojourn in Greenwich; in fact, there are picture postal cards of this house, which claim the honor for it. But this claim is denied by the Greenwich historians who say that the house in question was the Dan Bowen house, now destroyed, on the east side of Market Square. To settle this argument which raged for decades, the late Charles Ewing left a statement in affadavit form that his great-grandfather, Thomas Ewing, M.D., had told his grandson, James Josiah, the father of the affiant, that the tea was stored in and taken from the Dan Bowen house. Since Doctor Ewing was one of the principals in the tea party, this handed-down statement should effectively settle the question.

However, the Judy Husted house was the home of Henry "Tea" Stacks, who did not have far to go with his own improvised store house, carrying the tea in his pants and shoes, since the Market Square is only a few yards away.

The Market Square contains the handsome marble monument erected in 1908 in memory of the tea burners. On the sides of the monument are carved the names of the participants. A neat fence encloses it and the ground within is well-groomed and well-kept. Alongside the Square the road runs to Greenwich Pier; the same road that was originally planned to cut through where the Ewing house now stands and is the last road to debouch either east or west from the Great Street.

Across the intersection to the south is the Reeve-Rinehart house, a substantial brick building of unknown age. Mark Reeve owned the ground in 1682. The present owners are Mr. and Mrs. Phelps Rinehart and the long history in between is uncertain. The wall cupboards in this house are exquisite pieces of workmanship and the window panes are still the original, whatever the date may have been of construction.

Next to the Rinehart house is the last residence on the west side of the street. This is a fine modern brick mansion erected in 1913, the home of Miss Mary Goodwin, which is a treasure house of antique heirlooms. Her family was one of the first to settle in Greenwich.

On the east side of the street topping the slight elevation above the Cohansey, is the massive brick structure of the Orthodox Friends Meeting House. The house was built in 1771. A thick stone wall encloses it, bearing the date 1843. It has not been used as a place of worship for some time past. Today, the Friends are placing the house and grounds in the keeping of the Cumberland County Historical Society. It will be used for meetings and for an additional place besides the Wood mansion to exhibit a portion of the historical relics belonging to that society.

Only a short distance now and the Great Street has run its course. The wharf and the bend of the Cohansey are reached but first, before one comes actually to the creek, there is with its back to the town and sideways to the street, facing the creek, the Mark Reeve-John Sheppard house, probably the oldest house in Greenwich. This structure is built in three parts, each one progressively larger than its neighbor. (Until recently there was a fourth addition, a storehouse that dated far back in colonial days, but that has been removed.)

The land on which the Reeve-Sheppard house stands is the second oldest lot sold on the Great Street by Fenwick's executors. Mark Reeve was the purchaser in 1686 and built the first part of this house in 1696. At his death in the early years of the eighteenth century, the property passed to Joseph Browne, who dealt in river trade with a full-rigged sloop—one of the first on either creek or river. Browne did well, for his personal inventory showed that he had accumulated 142 ounces of silver plate, six Negro slaves and an Indian boy slave, and three houses.

The next owner was Thomas Chalkley, an early Quaker minister, whose Journal is a rare and excellent source book of historic information, especially appertaining to the Society of Friends. In 1726 he recounts, "the malignant distemper which prevailed at Cohansie," telling that from it more than seventy persons died.

Following Chalkley came the John Sheppard family, whose progeny is one of the largest in South Jersey. John Sheppard was a descendant of Thomas Sheppard of Tipperary, Ireland. Four brothers, Thomas, John, James and David came to America in the early 1680's, settling first at Shrewsbury in Monmouth County, East Jersey. In 1683 the four of them moved down to Greenwich, settled here permanently and purchased a part of the neck near the Cohansey, on the Fairfield or eastern side, which they named Shrewsbury Neck in honor of the Monmouth County town.

John Sheppard acquired the property and in 1734 built an addition which is marked with that date. (Another addition to the east was built in 1860.) The door of the central portion of this house has two fine "bull's eyes" of green glass set in the uppermost panel. In the interior is a glass china closet above a closed fire place with large and small cupboards on either side.

The Reeve-Sheppard house faces directly on Cohansey Creek and due to a bend in the stream the east side likewise faces the water. Its windows, its elegant bull's-eye doorway looked out on the brig Greyhound moored at anchor that December of 1774. It has seen much other maritime history as well. Here was the ferry originally contracted for 999 years by John Sheppard, which besides being the main artery of commercial travel, carried countless Quakers, Presbyterians and Baptists from the east, or Fairfield side, to worship at Greenwich. Here landed the stranded British seamen which the Spanish privateer released in 1748 after its piratical adventures in the Delaware; here also, under the darkest cover of night, small boats carrying blue and yellow signal lights, the nautical emblem of the "Underground Railway," landed fugitive slaves from the State of Delaware; here passed in broad daylight, on a fine spring day in 1861, a river steamer from Bridgeton, carrying the Cumberland County boys to the gory battlefields of the Civil War.

Now, the dock and the creek lie idle, save for a few fishing craft and power boats. In epitome and in remembrance, these lines:

> *"Here, by the forsaken Cohansey dock*
> *Where Greyhound lay, and pirate privateer,*
> *In livelier days; Forgotten, now, unsung*
> *Stand, Traveller, and Know*
> *That Father Time has stopped his Clock."*

Chapter Five

OF THE BROAD FIELDS

"Bacon's Adventure girds Cohansey
Broad the fields around it lie,
Moseley's Shield and Vauxhall Gardens
Names that were not born to die.
Mark, the Lords of Manor coming,
To new homes across the seas
Settling in their spacious acres
Near the town that burned the tea.

Sharing Boston's glory with it
In an act, defiant, bold
Written on the page of history
Of a gallant story told.
Here, where winds the old Cohansey
Tortuous, twisting towards the sea
Bacon's Venture still stands sentinel
To the town that burned the tea."

Past the Wood mansion on the right and the old 1795 store on the left, Bacon's Neck street runs west from a dead end on "Ye Greate Streete" to open country and to one of the most noted manorial tracts of Fenwick's

Colony. For this is the road to Bacon's Adventure, 260-acre tract of Samuel Bacon, Quaker who settled here in 1682. Time has changed the high sounding title "Adventure" into a plainer, shorter word, "Neck."

One of this nation's Anglo-Saxon heritages, now somewhat forgotten and neglected, is the preservation of place names. The English lords of the manor had high sounding and melodious names for their estates. The first settlers of Fenwick's Colony were not to the manor born; they were middle class artisans and business men who had invested their life savings in American real estate. Now, masters of their own plantations in this new world and immensely proud of their possessions, they gave their new estates names redolent of the land from which they came. For Samuel Bacon in particular, it was an adventure; happily he so named his acres.

The titles of the estates in Fenwick's Colony suggest, as no other means will do, the charm of English nomenclature. They sound much more like England than of the new world. Samples of this nomenclature of estates, the greater part of which are in the parent county of Salem, are: "Lumle's Sawley, Tyndale's Bowery, Watson's Ranthorpe, Provoes Holt, Paynes Pytle, Amwellbury, Hancock's Hurst, White's Dene, Bradfield, Beriton Fields, Hollybourne, Grundel Hill, Lefevre's Chase, Hedge Field, Page's Plantation, Braithwaite Hall, Petersfield, Webb's Arladon, Sandyburr Wood, Pilesgrove, Brothers Forest, Crawkerne Wood, Craven's "Choyce," and White's Vineyard. In the Greenwich-Cohansey section there are Bacon's Adventure, HasleField, Mannor Neck, Moseley's Shield, Vauxhall Gardens and Bethel. Moseley's Shield derived its name from Thomas Smyth who came from Moseley, Parish of Chadleton, Staffordshire, England. He added the word "Shield," undoubtedly to show the trappings of heraldry as well as to remember his old home. Moseley's Shield is now the Shrewsbury Neck section lying south and east of the Cohansey.

Bacon's Neck Street before it reaches open country is well built up with

---

houses, most of them very old. Two deserve special attention. On the left, going west, the third house from the store corner is the three-story frame with the tiny ancient leanto, the Stiles-Sheppard house. This house is an antiquarian's paradise. The cellar rafters are hand-hewn. The first floor, which was originally two rooms, contains a double fireplace, but the partition was later removed to give the family more living room space. There is a smoke house in the attic. Like most colonial homes, especially in the Greenwich section, the colonists cured or smoked their own hams and venison. The smoke-blackened timbers of side wall and roof attest to this old custom. The reason why this smoke closet was at the top of the house was simply that the residents figured that fumes would go out quicker from the attic and not smoke up the entire house.

The age of the old house is doubtful. It was probably built before the Revolution, and 1765 would be a fairly accurate guess. It has had various names: the Stiles, the Billy Sheppard, the Gibe, the Charley Sheppard and now the Leon Glaspey (the present owner who bought it from Charles E. Sheppard of Collingswood, New Jersey).

Opposite is a two-story brick house, stuccoed over on the front, now rather woebegone in appearance, which bears on its west wall the date of erection—1765—and the initials P. H. D. standing for Phillip and Hannah Dennis, the builders.

Samuel Bacon settled first at Woodbridge, East Jersey, then in 1682 bought 260 acres from John Adams, the son-in-law of John Fenwick, and immediately moved to his "Venture." After the meticulous honest way of the Quakers, Bacon bought his land twice, the second purchase being from two Indian chiefs, Shawkamum and Ethoe. This included the land he got from Adams, and some additional, bringing his total acreage to 400, although some of the land involved in the two transactions overlapped. For the land which the Indians called Cotanangut, Bacon gave the Indians "two coats of Dussols, three blankets, two handfulls of powder, six bars of lead, two knives, two pairs of stockings, two looking glasses, two hoes, two axes, two needles, two awls, one gun, one guilder in wampum and two pairs of scissors."

The deed for Bacon's Adventure was mislaid for many years. About 1905, in a title search, it came to light and was preserved as a historic relic by the County Historical society, until a recent year when tragic to relate someone removed it from the society's archives. The deed was made of stiff parchment and bore the marks of the Indian chiefs; the seals were made of leather with red sealing wax attached.

Bacon, like all other settlers, first built a log cabin, or at least a small timber structure. Then as he became more affluent, he built a brick house. The manor house of the Adventure burned in about 1862 but the house was rebuilt and is now the farm house on the center of the old manor tract in Bacon's Neck.

The proximity of the Adventure to the Delaware River made it accessible for foraging and marauding expeditions on the part of the British whose fleet lay in the river for a good part of the war. The *Pennsylvania Weekly Advertiser* gives this account of a raid, on May 6, 1776, the facts being supplied by an American militia officer:

"This serves to inform you of an alarm we had about eleven o'clock this day, of a party of regulars, landing on Tindall's Island in Bacon's Neck, about four miles from Greenwich; supposed to be about thirty in number; shooting down the cattle; taking them on board, etc., whereupon I called the militia together as soon as possible, and upon our appearance, a gun was fired from on board one of the vessels, for them to repair on board, which they did with the greatest precipitation. Our men pursued so closely that we were near taking three of them prisoners, one of whom left an excellent musket behind which we got with some cartridges.

Ewing, Bacon, Gallagher House, built in 1765.

Seeley House.

"They hollowed to our men to go on board the King Fisher, and they would pay for the beef. It is supposed they took off between 20 and 30 head of cattle, 5 they left dead on the shore, and wounded many more, which with all the rest we have drove from the water side. They have taken this morning a shallop belonging to Daniel Richards, bound from Philadelphia to Morris river, but the hands escaped to shore."—

South of the rebuilt modern home on Bacon's Adventure, the Neck road forks. The left fork takes one past the frame William Bacon house with a fine fanlight over its main doorway, continues on past one more aged frame farmhouse, known as the Hannah Taylor farm, date about 1730, and finally ends in the fast land by the Cohansey. At this point Samuel Bacon probably landed to explore and settle his new Manor of Bacon's Adventure. Here, Joseph Hancock erected a small summer cottage from whose porch may clearly be seen across the intervening three-fourths of a mile of open space, the small ship and fishing boat harbor of Greenwich Piers and beyond that the long stretched out, red brick facade of Greenwich Town.

The right fork of the Neck road leads to Nancy's Island on Cabin Creek, a remotely accessible tributary of the creek where Captain William Kidd is supposed to have hidden some of his treasure.

Retracing our steps up the Bacon's Neck road to the intersection of the street coming out of Greenwich, and continuing north, on the left is an old rough cast house known as the Brown, which is well over two hundred years old. On the same side but further north and set in a grove of trees is the spacious mansion of Gabriel Davis. It was built of brick in 1785 and carries the initials of husband and wife, G. S. D., on the gable peak. Of late this place is called the McAllister farm. It is a huge structure, the walls of which are said to be fifteen inches thick. The interior is vast and high-ceilinged; high mantels above the fireplaces somewhat suggest that the house would have been of better design for a city mansion than for a house on the lonely fastland of Bacon's Adventure. The house contains two out-of-the-ordinary antique features: one is the heavy ancient hardware and the lever bar on the inside of the main door; and the other a finely done corner cupboard which has a shelf that may be pulled out on a slide and is used to hold a decanter and glasses.

Gabriel Davis, who built the house in 1785 and married Sarah Miller, died without issue. The property passed to a nephew, Ebenezer Hall, and for many years was referred to as the Hall homestead. The doings and "carryings on" of Gabriel have found there way into local folklore. He was a very wealthy man. There was some suspicion that his material gains in the shape of gold and silver coins accrued from certain activity on his part which might come under the head of "trading with the enemy." The Revolution was on, the British fleet lay close, the nights were dark, and it was not far to the river. There were many tongues wagging. When Gabriel lay dying, with the assembled family mourning by his bedside, there suddenly came into the room a strange black dog, which no one had ever seen before. The dog jumped up on the bed alongside Gabriel. The horrified family made motions to push it off but the sick man restrained them. "No," he said. "Let it stay, it will go when I die." And when he did die a few hours later, the dog jumped off the bed, went out the bedroom door and was never seen again.

On a diagonal from the Davis house is the Sheppard-Hancock house. In the rear of this house which fronts southeast may be seen parts of the old railroad bed which ran one-and-one-half miles to Bayside. Also, here where Tappan Lane debouches to the left and to the Bay from the main Bacon's Neck road once stood the Bacon's Neck flag station of the Central Railroad of New Jersey. Years ago, palatial coaches of the railroad rolled down the track between the Davis-Hall and the Sheppard-Hancock house enroute to Bayside, sometime called Caviar. This now overgrown roadbed with rotting ties was part of a certain railroad magnate's dream of empire to connect New York and Washington by means of rail ferry connections across the Hudson, Delaware and Cheseapeake. The dream was completely unrealized; even a flurry of business in the 1890's, marketing caviar from Bayside, failed to keep this south Jersey division of the CRRNJ solvent. With the advent of the auto, the passenger service of the road died out altogether. Since 1935, the rails have been torn up. Now the Central is complete only to Bridgeton and Bowentown, running from Jersey City its eastern terminal. The railroad stations of Bayside, Bacon's Neck, Greenwich and Sheppard's Mills are now only memories.

With its back to the old roadbed, facing southeast, is the brick and frame Sheppard-Hancock house. Here again, is the familiar pattern of a higher part and a dropped wing, both having front entrance doors. It was built in 1750 and for many, many years has been known as the Sheppard house. No less than five generations of Sheppards have owned it, including the present owner, Joseph Hancock, whose mother was a Sheppard.

The Hancock house, to differentiate from the many Sheppard houses in Greenwich, has had some additions of frame to its original brick portion. The whole exterior ensemble is a well-kept, well-groomed affair with a spacious terrace in front. The interior, like many other Greenwich homes, is an antiquarian's paradise. There is an exquisite china closet, one of the finest pieces of skilled workmanship dating from colonial days that this compiler has ever seen. There is an immense fireplace with its original wide boarded pine panelling. There are ancient pieces of hardware still in use, hand-hewn beams with axe marks still visible, innumerable pieces of antique furniture, an elegant front doorway with a straight four-part divided fanlight.

Tappan's Lane runs to Bayside and Delaware Bay, where by this time, unlike the river at Trenton or at Philadelphia, one cannot see across to the other side. In the last fast land before the marshes, on Tappan's Lane and close by, are two colonial houses. The house on the Lane nearest Bayside is known as the Maul house; the one nearer Greenwich is called the Glaspell farm. Both these houses, now remodelled, were built by Sheppards before the revolution. This family has contributed many colonial dwelling houses to Greenwich. Because this particular branch of the Sheppard family were Seventh Day Baptists, who observed Saturday as a day of rest instead of Sunday, Tappan's Lane was often called Seventh Day Lane. These two properties are now owned by the Bonham family.

Off Tappan's Lane on a side road to the northwest about a half mile from the Davis-Hall and Sheppard-Hancock houses, and visible from both when the foliage is not too thick, is one of the architectural gems of early Greenwich. It is a beautiful hipped specimen with a gambrel roof. This is a Dennis house, having been erected about 1720 by Phillip Dennis, a large landowner on Bacon's Neck. The front has the usual Flemish bond design of header and stretcher brick in red and blue. The entire east side has been covered with gray mortar, some of which has peeled exposing the ancient brick work beneath. An extremely large oven in the Dennis house is said to have produced many loaves of bread for the Cumberland County militia stationed in and around Greenwich during the Revolutionary days. In the short span of a few years, time has placed a heavy hand on this once magnificent colonial glazed-brick structure. Hillbillies and age have combined to render it in such condition that its span can not be much longer.

Past the Bacon's Neck school house, which was organized in 1801 (the present frame school dates back to 1911), and the airport, one of the few modern notes in or around Greenwich, the trail leads left on the cross roads near the airfield. Then after a short distance, right down a turning twisting lane to end up at the Morris Goodwin house. This elegant mansion was erected about 1800 and is set in the middle of a large 300-acre tract. Here are spacious windows, doors with brass knockers, a lovely fanlight over the main doorway, good mantel pieces (handcarved), and ivy on the walls. But its crowning glory is the kitchen, so gigantic that oxen were trained to come in and haul the backlog to the massive fireplace. And it may be added that this statement is neither folklore nor tradition, but fact.

From this house, situated on a slight elevation, there is an excellent view of the river and bay.

This is also a Sheppard house, but the builder, Thomas Sheppard, died before it could be completed. A Mrs. Mary White bought the unfinished mansion and completed it. Mary White, whose maiden name was Thompson, had quite a career, including, as it did, three marriages. Her first was to Thomas Sheppard, who it is said she chose from among the militia which marched down the Great Street of Greenwich when the Americans defended the line of the Cohansey Creek in March of 1778. Soldier Sheppard died and she married Samuel Silver. Their son, Thomas Silver, patented the first steam governor. After Silver died, she married William White and as Mrs. White bought this tract. A wide branch of Stow Creek, which divides Salem from Cumberland County, flows past this estate, a stream large enough for vessels to have landed building material for the house.

For a long time after the death of Mary Thompson Sheppard Silver White the estate was in possession of the Mark Harmer family (which gave its name to the hamlet of Harmersville in Salem County). Morris Goodwin married into the Harmer family. His grandson, with the same name is the present owner.

North and west of here, and reached by devious, winding roads, lies

---

115

Stathem's Neck. This land is bordered by marsh and by the waters of Stow Creek which empties into the Delaware by the now forgotten railroad terminal of Bayside-Caviar. In 1690, Thomas Stathem bought about 600 acres in this Neck and paid quit rents for it to the heirs of John Fenwick. Two more Stathem brothers, Zebulon and Phillip, followed Thomas and acquired more land in this immediate section. From these three progenitors, the Stathem family became quite numerous in Greenwich and the name therefore was prominent for decades.

A brick colonial house built by the Stathems still stands on the back road through the Neck which leads to Flax Point. Here is another haunt. Aaron Stathem, who lived here throughout the revolutionary years, was an ardent Tory and made no bones about it. His wife was said to be an ardent Whig who disapproved of her husband's traffic with the enemy. Unlike his neighbor, Gabriel Davis, Stathem announced his politics, but like Gabriel he would, under cover of night, take dressed, cured meat by small boat to the waiting British vessels in the River, and receive gold coin in payment thereof. In his house Aaron had built a mantel piece over the fire place that would lift up. Into this bin he would dump his British acquired gold. One night his wife entered the room to find him busily engaged in unloading a large pile of coins. Knowing where it came from, she registered her feelings by gathering up her skirts and "swishing" out of the room. Some say that even now, if you can get close enough to the lonely Stathem house at Flax Point, and if you have good ears, you may still hear the angry "swish" of Madam Stathem's skirts.

Turning east about two miles from Stathem's Point, on the road to Head of Greenwich, there is an old frame house so remodelled that its age is not patent to the outside observer. It is a Ewing property and goes back to 1718 and possibly earlier. The original, or 1718 part, stood across the road but was moved from that location well over a century ago and another wing added to it. In the parlor is a Franklin stove, invented by none other than Benjamin Franklin in 1742. It is made of iron, open faced, within an iron hearth extending out into the room. Instead of patenting it, Franklin gave it away, declaring, "that as we enjoy advantages from the inventions of others, we should be glad of an opportunity to serve others with an invention of ours."

From the Ewings the place passed to the Sheppards, Harmers, Bacons, Glaspeys and into the possession of J. W. Butler. Glaspey rebuilt some more and fixed up the back part of the house with a new addition. In an upper west room was a door opening into a north room. When owner Glaspey rebuilt the north room he had no use for the door but built against it, leaving it with the old heavy hinges and bolts. Thus, it would open about two inches against the wall of the next room and it also opened the way for another ghost, because people sleeping in the room declared that they beheld a demure little Quaker lady, complete with gray shawl and bonnet, step out from behind this door and stand silently at the head of the bed for several minutes before departing into the shadows from whence she had come. The property is now in possession of Philip Griffith.

The late Charles Ewing, who lived and died in the mansion on Great Street, dubbed this early ancestral house of his family "Resurrection Hall," presumably because it was once moved from its original location and added to so often. One might be constrained to wonder, however, if knowing of the Quaker lady ghost, Mr. Ewing might have had another idea in mind.

Past Resurrection Hall and in an easterly direction, where the Bacon's Neck Road to Gum Tree Corner crosses the road from the Necks to North Greenwich, is Vauxhall Gardens. Like its fairly near neighbor, the Dennis house, this, too, is constructed of red and blue brick in Flemish bond, hipped and gambrel-roofed. It is in much better repair, at least to exterior view. There is a rather nondescript wooden addition on the western end of Vauxhall Gardens which, ancient as it may be, does not enhance the entire picture. The eastern or original brick part of Vauxhall Gardens, while pleasing to the eye, has suffered untold depredations within. Before the outside walls were painted and refinished by new owners, and while the interior lay open to all and sundry, impious vandal hands, in the guise of antique dealers, stripped the old house of its mantels and its paneling. These went to grace the home of a nouveau riche in a distant big city.

The Gardens were built by Thomas Maskell who emigrated from England to Connecticut in 1685. His son, Thomas, came to West Jersey, probably with the Fairfield Presbyterian emigration as early as 1700. Some time thereafter he built this house, which he was pleased to call Vauxhall Gardens after the fashionable and famous gardens in London.

North Greenwich is reached at the distance of a mile from Vauxhall Gardens. Turning left on the old King's road to Salem for a few yards, another abrupt turn is made to the right to pursue what is known as "the straight road to Roadstown from North Greenwich." There is a colonial house on the left about one mile from N. Greenwich. Close by on the right is a magnificent structure dated 1783, which has been completely restored and added to. This house on the right is now known as the Lupton-Mills house; the builders initials are B.R.R., standing for Richard and Rebecca Bacon.

Magnificent shade and well kept lawns add to the beauty of the Lupton-Mills house, which is easily one of the show places of Greenwich. The house on the left is a Tyler property, one of many built by that family in the two counties of Salem and Cumberland. Situated on a knoll, the most interesting thing about this 1786 edifice is that the main entrance hall, after the grand manner of Virginia plantations, extends north

Bond House. Erected in 1725 as Rectory for Saint Stephens Episcopal Church.

Tea-Burners' Monument in Market Square.

to south throughout the house, insuring a breeze even in extremely hot weather. Alas, a recent alteration tore out the hallway of cooling breezes.

From the view afforded by the elevation at these two houses, one may see the Delaware River as it widens out into the Bay and also the several light houses, including the famous Ship John Light.

At this point, a retrace is needed back to the Salem road and then a bit north until the Arthur Davis mill (now not used) and millpond are reached. It is the Macanippuck which forms the pond. Here is the magnificent Richard Seeley house, the upright portion of which was built in 1816. There are two smaller brick parts, the smallest of which could be very old, for this is the site of the Gibbon grist mill. Undoubtedly the Gibbons built a home for their miller back in the early 1700's. The crowning glory of the Seeley mansion is its parlor fireplace with an exquisite handcarved mantel above it. The Seeleys were very prominent in Cumberland County history; one, Elias P., was governor of New Jersey in 1833.

Left on the down grade approaching Roadstown, set in a swale of a small valley, is a two story brick structure known as the "hospital" house. The date of erection is approximately 1760 and it was owned by Doctor Elijah Bowen, a surgeon of revolutionary days. In seeking for the solution as to why this house should be called the hospital house, for there is some local mystery about it, it must not be forgotten that when the Salem and Cumberland County militia were defeated by the British in the engagements of Quinton's Bridge and Hancock's Bridge, respectively March 18th and 21st, 1778, they retreated from the line of the Alloways Creek to the line of the Cohansey. In all human probability they brought their wounded with them, their casualties having been quite severe, and may have stopped at this house.

From Roadstown-Greenwich on March 28th, 1778, a long and pathetic appeal for help was sent to General George Washington at Valley Forge, thru channels via Colonel Israel Shreve at Haddonfield, asking for immediate reinforcements and pointing out the salient and pertinent fact that if the enemy should penetrate to that area the "bread basket" of the American army would be lost. This poignant, truthful appeal calls attention to a long forgotten fact in American history: In February of 1778, Mad Anthony Wayne had secured enough cattle, food, and forage in the two counties of Salem and Cumberland alone to keep alive the tatterdemalion army, facetiously known as "Grand," which had been slowly starving to death on the bleak hillsides near Norristown.

This appeal for help to Washington was signed by twelve civil and eleven military officers of the two counties' militia. Since many of them were Cohansey men, of Greenwich, Roadstown and the Bridge, and some of them were afterwards famous, the list is given in entirety: (Civil), Joseph Newcomb, Joel Fithian, Samuel Leake, Nathan Leake, Ephraim Mills, John Holme, Providence Ludlam, John Peck, Jonathan Bowen, Ananias Sayre, Ebenezer Howell, and Jonathan Elmer (one of the first two United States senators from New Jersey); (Military), Elijah Hand, Benjamin Holme, Silas Newcomb (these first three were colonels and Newcomb became a brigadier general at a later period), Abijah Holme, Samuel Ogden, Thomas Ewing, Edward Hall, Daniel Maskell, Henry Sparks, Robert Patterson and Enos Seeley.

Colonel Shreve forwarded the appeal to General Washington, adding his own urgent appeal for more troops stating a true but deplorable fact: that the line of the Cohansey which stretched from the Dennis house near Bayside, through Greenwich, to Roadstown was manned by only three hundred men armed only with fowling pieces and certainly too weak to withstand the two regular British regiments that Colonel Charles Mawhood and Major John Graves Simcoe had under their command at Salem and on the line of the Alloways, scarcely ten miles distant. But by

April, the question of more troops for the colonists fortunately became an academic one, since the British withdrew from Salem and in two months more evacuated Philadelphia to return to New York. Had they elected to attack the American militia on the line of the Cohansey, there would have been no reinforcements for the militia simply because Washington had absolutely no manpower available to send them.

It is two miles from the Head of Greenwich to Roadstown. This tiny hamlet, its houses stretched along the respective four cross roads, are mostly modern homes of retired farmers; but there are two venerable houses here, both bearing the same date (1770) in glazed blue brick upon their walls. The one at the northwest corner is the Ananias Sayre house; the other just short of the southeast corner is the David Bowen house, whose builder was the last royal sheriff of Cumberland County. Roadstown, two centuries ago, was called Kingstown. To honor Ananias Sayre, a local patriot and judge, Kingstown was officially changed to Sayre Cross Roads, but it is more aptly named Roadstown, because the four principal roads from Shiloh, Bridgeton, Jericho-Salem and Greenwich cross here. It was from Roadstown that the military and civil officers made their appeal to Washington in 1778.

On the right, or eastern, road to Bridgeton there may be seen the beautiful early American brick church of the Baptists which was erected in 1803 but whose organized congregation goes back to 1690. It is especially revered by the Baptists because it is the Mother church of that faith in southern New Jersey.

To the north, a mile out of Roadstown on the left side, and about another mile from the Seventh Day colony of Baptists at Shiloh, is the Howell house. One of the many signs erected by the Cumberland County Historical Society to mark its historic sites gives a succinct account of its history. "This is the meeting place of the tea burners—174 years ago—(The sign was erected in 1948.) The house was built in 1770 by Ebenezer Howell—Home of Richard Howell, third Governor of New Jersey."

It has much more history than that: the Daughters of the Confederacy should be greatly interested in the fact that this was the birthplace of William Howell, father of Varina Howell who became Mrs. Jefferson Davis, the First Lady of the Confederate States.

The Howell house is long and low, not upright and tall as are so many of its colonial neighbors. It is painted yellow and it has all the care its antique-loving owners, Mr. and Mrs. Fred Renne, can give it. A sunburst china closet is the pride of the Howell house interior.

As the early evening shadows deepened on December 22nd, 1774, men by twos and threes and singly came into this house after tethering their horses, held a brief but secret meeting, came out in a body and began the four-mile ride that was their date with destiny. A mile to Roadstown, straight on past the intersection and the brand new brick houses of Sayre and Bowen, then hard by Elijah's Bowen's Hospital house, taking the east fork of the road, they headed for Greenwich. A quarter of a mile short of where this road runs dead end into the Great Street the cavalcade turned down a long lane to the left, and entered a two part, two story frame dwelling. Here, under the dynamic personality of their leader, the several young men smeared their faces with paint, donned Indian feathered head dresses, and thus accoutred, rode off a second time down Great Street for a rendezvous with history and to, literally, set America on fire. Much of the patriotic spirit of the Revolution caught flame that night, fanned by the conflagration of the tea on the Market Square in Greenwich.

This last house still stands, a true shrine for every American to visit who values his birthright. This was the birthplace and the home of Phillip Vickers Fithian. And here, appropriately enough, ends the tour of the old houses and of the history of Greenwich.

———

"And for brows to wear the Myrtle
Place this garland, here and now
For a native son of Greenwich
Who chose the pulpit, than the plough.
Preacher, prophet, soldier, writer,
He, whose farflung vision could Foresee;
Write Fithian's name in Golden Letters,
In the town that burned the tea."

———

125